Noel Scott
Eric Laws
Editors

D0223889

Knowledge Sharing and Quality Assurance in Hospitality and Tourism

Knowledge Sharing and Quality Assurance in Hospitality and Tourism has been co-published simultaneously as *Journal of Quality Assurance in Hospitality & Tourism*, Volume 7, Numbers 1/2 2006.

*Pre-publication
REVIEWS,
COMMENTARIES,
EVALUATIONS . . .*

"This FRESH AND INNOVATIVE perspective on tourism combines an exploration of the social context within which knowledge sharing occurs and the more established analysis of managing knowledge systems. In addressing the previous neglect of knowledge management by tourism researchers, the work brings together examples from diverse geographic settings and contexts. The collection WILL BE GREATLY WELCOMED BY BOTH SCHOLARS AND INDUSTRY PRACTITIONERS."

Brian King, PhD
*Professor and Head
School of Hospitality,
Tourism and Marketing
Victoria University, Australia*

More pre-publication
REVIEWS, COMMENTARIES, EVALUATIONS . . .

"I APPLAUD THE EDITORS of this volume for firstly recognizing the need to explore in greater detail the significance of this vitally important issue and secondly for crafting a book that brings together an excellent range of chapters that explore a wide variety of knowledge issues. This book FILLS A SIGNIFICANT GAP in the understanding of knowledge and its applications. Readers will benefit from the insights provided as well as gain understanding through the case studies presented. I RECOMMEND THIS BOOK to fellow academics, students and practitioners who are interested in learning more about the role, power and maintenance of knowledge in the tourism industry."

Bruce Prideaux, PhD
*Professor of Marketing
and Tourism Management
James Cook University, Australia*

THHP

The Haworth Hospitality Press®
An Imprint of The Haworth Press, Inc.

Knowledge Sharing
and Quality Assurance
in Hospitality and Tourism

Knowledge Sharing and Quality Assurance in Hospitality and Tourism has been co-published simultaneously as *Journal of Quality Assurance in Hospitality & Tourism*, Volume 7, Numbers 1/2 2006.

Monographic Separates from the *Journal of Quality Assurance in Hospitality & Tourism™*

For additional information on these and other Haworth Press titles, including descriptions, tables of contents, reviews, and prices, use the QuickSearch catalog at http://www.HaworthPress.com.

Knowledge Sharing
and Quality Assurance
in Hospitality and Tourism

Noel Scott
Eric Laws
Editors

Knowledge Sharing and Quality Assurance in Hospitality and Tourism has been co-published simultaneously as *Journal of Quality Assurance in Hospitality & Tourism*, Volume 7, Numbers 1/2 2006.

The Haworth Hospitality Press®
An Imprint of The Haworth Press, Inc.

New York • London • Victoria (AU)
www.HaworthPress.com

FEB 0 5 2007

DOUGLAS COLLEGE LIBRARY

Published by

The Haworth Hospitality Press®, 10 Alice Street, Binghamton, NY 13904-1580 USA

The Haworth Hospitality Press® is an imprint of The Haworth Press, Inc., 10 Alice Street, Binghamton, NY 13904-1580 USA.

Knowledge Sharing and Quality Assurance in Hospitality and Tourism has been co-published simultaneously as *Journal of Quality Assurance in Hospitality & Tourism*, Volume 7, Numbers 1/2 2006.

© 2006 by The Haworth Press, Inc. All rights reserved. No part of this work may be reproduced or utilized in any form or by any means, electronic or mechanical, including photocopying, microfilm and recording, or by any information storage and retrieval system, without permission in writing from the publisher. Printed in the United States of America.

The development, preparation, and publication of this work has been undertaken with great care. However, the publisher, employees, editors, and agents of The Haworth Press and all imprints of The Haworth Press, Inc., including The Haworth Medical Press® and Pharmaceutical Products Press®, are not responsible for any errors contained herein or for consequences that may ensue from use of materials or information contained in this work. With regard to case studies, identities and circumstances of individuals discussed herein have been changed to protect confidentiality. Any resemblance to actual persons, living or dead, is entirely coincidental.

The Haworth Press is committed to the dissemination of ideas and information according to the highest standards of intellectual freedom and the free exchange of ideas. Statements made and opinions expressed in this publication do not necessarily reflect the views of the Publisher, Directors, management, or staff of The Haworth Press, Inc., or an endorsement by them.

Cover design by Jennifer Gaska

Library of Congress Cataloging-in-Publication Data

Knowledge sharing and quality assurance in hospitality and tourism / Noel Scott, Eric Laws, editors.
    p. cm.
    "Co-published simultaneously as Journal of Quality Assurance in Hospitality & Tourism, Volume 7, Numbers 1/2 2006."
    Includes bibliographical references and index.
    ISBN-13: 978-0-7890-3411-3 (hard cover : alk. paper)
    ISBN-10: 0-7890-3411-5 (hard cover : alk. paper)
    ISBN-13: 978-0-7890-3412-0 (soft cover : alk. paper)
    ISBN-10: 0-7890-3412-3 (soft cover : alk. paper)
    1. Hospitality industry–Quality control. 2. Tourism–Quality control. 3. Knowledge management. I. Scott, Noel, 1958- II. Laws, Eric, 1945-

TX911.3.Q34K66 2006
647.94068'5–dc22

2006013852

Indexing, Abstracting & Website/Internet Coverage

This section provides you with a list of major indexing & abstracting services and other tools for bibliographic access. That is to say, each service began covering this periodical during the year noted in the right column. Most Websites which are listed below have indicated that they will either post, disseminate, compile, archive, cite or alert their own Website users with research-based content from this work. (This list is as current as the copyright date of this publication.)

Abstracting, Website/Indexing Coverage . . . . Year When Coverage Began

- *(CAB ABSTRACTS, CABI) Available in print, diskettes updated weekly, and on INTERNET. Providing full bibliographic listings, author affiliation, augmented keyword searching <http://www.cabi.org>* **2006**

- *(IBZ) International Bibliography of Periodical Literature on the Humanities and Social Sciences (Thomson) <http://www.saur.de>.* **2000**

- *Biological Sciences Database (Cambridge Scientific Abstracts) <http://www.csa.com>* **2006**

- *Cabell's Directory of Publishing Opportunities in Management > (Bibliographic Access) <http://www.cabells.com/>* **2006**

- *Cambridge Scientific Abstracts (A leading publisher of scientific information in print journals, online databases, CD-ROM and via the Internet.) <http://www.csa.com>* **2006**

- *CIRET (Centre International de Recherches et d'Etudes Touristiques). Computerized Tourism & General Bibliography <http://www.ciret-tourism.com>* **2000**

- *EBSCOhost Electronic Journals Service (EJS) <http://www.ejournals.ebsco.com>* **2001**

- *Elsevier Eflow -D <http://www.elsevier.com>* **2006**

(continued)

(continued)

Special Bibliographic Notes related to special journal issues (separates) and indexing/abstracting:

- indexing/abstracting services in this list will also cover material in any "separate" that is co-published simultaneously with Haworth's special thematic journal issue or DocuSerial. Indexing/abstracting usually covers material at the article/chapter level.
- monographic co-editions are intended for either non-subscribers or libraries which intend to purchase a second copy for their circulating collections.
- monographic co-editions are reported to all jobbers/wholesalers/approval plans. The source journal is listed as the "series" to assist the prevention of duplicate purchasing in the same manner utilized for books-in-series.
- to facilitate user/access services all indexing/abstracting services are encouraged to utilize the co-indexing entry note indicated at the bottom of the first page of each article/chapter/contribution.
- this is intended to assist a library user of any reference tool (whether print, electronic, online, or CD-ROM) to locate the monographic version if the library has purchased this version but not a subscription to the source journal.
- individual articles/chapters in any Haworth publication are also available through The Haworth Document Delivery Service (HDDS).

Knowledge Sharing
and Quality Assurance
in Hospitality and Tourism

CONTENTS

ABOUT THE EDITORS

Noel Scott is a lecturer at the School of Tourism and Leisure Management, The University of Queensland, Australia. He holds a PhD from the University of Queensland. Prior to his academic career, he was a senior government tourism planning and strategy manager. Noel Scott's research interests involve strategic management and marketing. Within this area he has conducted research into the organization structure of tourism in Australia, the dynamics of new types of tourism products and new product development, planning and management of tourism organizations and destinations as well as extensive market research into tourism visitors. He has also worked as a consultant on a number of tourism consultancy projects for the private sector.

Eric Laws is Adjunct Professor of Tourism Services at James Cook University, Cairns, Australia. Eric has a PhD from Griffith University, an MPhil from the University of Surrey and an MA from Thames Polytechnic. He has written and edited several books on various aspects of Tourism Management, and published many papers on tourism service quality, destination management, structural relations in the tourism industry and crisis management.

ALL HAWORTH HOSPITALITY PRESS
BOOKS AND JOURNALS ARE PRINTED
ON CERTIFIED ACID-FREE PAPER

Knowledge Sharing
in Tourism and Hospitality

Noel Scott

Eric Laws

What does it mean for an industry to adopt a 'knowledge-based' platform? While the concept appears logical, the actual path to better creation and utilization of knowledge is less clear. Prior authors have discussed developing a knowledge approach as a necessity for tourism organizations to be competitive (Cooper, 2005; Jafari, 1990). This is because the context for individual companies and the industry includes operating in conditions of increasing uncertainty, shorter product life cycles, rapidly developing technologies and more intrusive regulatory constraints. Knowledge management (KM) is seen to be an important response. "To adapt to continuously changing business conditions and to generate innovations, companies need to acquire new market knowledge, administer and exploit their knowledge stock and share knowledge across organisational entities. . . In short, companies need to engage in knowledge management" (Schlegelmilch & Penz, 2002). Knowledge is considered a company's most valuable resource (Buckley & Carter, 2002; Zack, 1999b) and also an individual's source of employment opportunities (Kodama, 2005). Tourism destinations have been enjoined to develop knowledge infrastructure (Cooper, 2002). The seminal econ-

[Haworth co-indexing entry note]: "Knowledge Sharing in Tourism and Hospitality." Scott, Noel, and Eric Laws. Co-published simultaneously in Journal of Quality Assurance in Hospitality & Tourism (The Haworth Hospitality Press, an imprint of The Haworth Press, Inc.) Vol. 7, No. 1/2, 2006, pp. 1-12; and: Knowledge Sharing and Quality Assurance in Hospitality and Tourism (ed: Noel Scott and Eric Laws) The Haworth Hospitality Press, an imprint of The Haworth Press, Inc., 2006, pp. 1-12. Single or multiple copies of this article are available for a fee from The Haworth Document Delivery Service [1-800-HAWORTH, 9:00 a.m. - 5:00 p.m. (EST). E-mail address: docdelivery@haworthpress.com].

Available online at http://jqaht.haworthpress.com
© 2006 by The Haworth Press, Inc. All rights reserved.
doi:10.1300/J162v07n01_01

1

omist Alfred Marshall characterised knowledge as the most powerful engine of production (Marshall, 1890).

Clearly, knowledge exists in varying forms with different levels of accessibility and ownership. Polanyi (1958) distinguished three levels of personal knowledge; the skills of an individual, acting in a social context, and expertise, the ability to influence the rules and domain of knowledge. Much of the current discussion of knowledge however revolves around ownership and use of knowledge at the group level. Thus the contemporary interest in knowledge management expands the discussion to its importance to companies and industries. Bill Gates of Microsoft (Gates & Hemmingway, 1999) used the phrase "corporate IQ" to emphasise the point that corporate knowledge is more than the sum of knowledge held by individuals involved in a company. He argued that a smart company with a high corporate IQ is one where employees are not only intelligent and experienced, but also interact to learn from each other. This assumes openness and willingness to share knowledge and for implementation has far reaching implications for cultural change within an organization. Similarly, the discussion of industry clusters, learning regions and inter-organizational knowledge networks (Michael, 2003; Pechlaner, Abfalter, & Raich, 2002; Saxena, 2005) is based on the management of knowledge at a group level of analysis, and as several papers in this volume demonstrate, a large unit of analysis such as 'the destination' is often the most appropriate analytical scale when considering tourism.

Together the two notions; firstly that knowledge is important and vital to competition yet not well defined in its methodology, and secondly, that knowledge generally, and particularly in tourism needs to be considered from an interorganizational perspective were the genesis of this special issue. The combination of these two ideas led us to the topic of 'knowledge sharing' in tourism. Tourism as an industry and particularly at the destination level involves collaboration and simultaneous competition between the member organizations. It therefore provides a useful context for the study of knowledge sharing. In this introduction, we discuss some of the important concepts of knowledge and seek to relate them to the themes and ideas raised by our contributors.

DEFINITIONS OF KNOWLEDGE

Armistead and Meakins (2002) recommends that discussions of KM begin by addressing the question, "What is knowledge?" The answer seems to be that knowledge comes in many colours and types. Whitehill, (1997) for example, has suggested a typology of knowledge as: encoded knowledge (know what?), habitual knowledge (know how?), scientific knowledge (know why?), collaboration knowledge (know who?), process knowledge (know when and where?) and communal knowledge (care why?). Here, knowledge is defined in terms of information theory with the significance that it can be stored and manipulated (Fischer & Frohlich, 2001). However, this typology seems to ignore the ownership question. Another approach that embodies knowledge albeit at the individual level has been developed by Willke (1998) cited in Schlegelmilch and Penz (2002) who regards knowledge as information embedded in the context of system-specific patterns of experiences. Thus the components of knowledge include technical expertise, problem-solving capability, creativity and managerial skills which are embodied in the employees of the organization (Jordon & Jones, 1997). The belief in mind perspective deals with the cognitive status of knowing (Harris, 1996, cited in Schlegelmilch and Penz (2002); (Shin, Holden, & Schmidt, 2001)]. Personalised knowledge is the outcome of combining information (analysed data) with experience and context Context provides the individual's framework for understanding the world, e.g., social values, religion, heritage and gender (Harris, 1996, cited in Schlegelmilch and Penz, 2002).

At a company level, Zack (1999a) differentiates between three types of knowledge. Core knowledge is the basic understanding of its industry by a company. Advanced knowledge is the basis for differentiation by companies within a certain industry. Companies with innovative knowledge strongly influence the dynamics of the industry by developing innovative products while competitors strive to adapt. Here the application of knowledge involves knowing and acting simultaneously (Shin et al., 2001; Zack, 1999b) and therefore who is doing the acting is important. Knowledge as a process is "rooted in the view of the organization as a knowledge system and knowledge as competitive resources" (Shin et al., 2001:348). The idea that knowledge involves action is discussed by Nonaka and Takeuchi (1995) who regard justified belief and commitment as two key characteristics of knowledge.

Knowledge creation is driven by the flow of information, anchored in the beliefs and commitment of its holder. An important distinction has been made between explicit knowledge which is formal and systematic and more easily shared with others compared to tacit knowledge. Tacit knowledge is highly personal, hard to formalise and thus difficult to communicate to others, and deeply rooted in action. Drucker (1999) regards knowledge worker productivity as poorly managed and therefore similar to that of manual labourers a hundred years ago. Here, again, we touch on issues of ownership and control. More positively, Nonaka et al. describe a "spiral of knowledge" to illustrate the process of creating knowledge in an organisation through the interaction between tacit and explicit knowledge (Nonaka, Reinmoeller, & Senoo, 1998; Nonaka, Toyama, & Konno, 2000). This also leads to the idea of mapping knowledge processing tasks to show where knowledge is located within a company and who needs specific knowledge.

STRATEGIC ASPECTS OF KNOWLEDGE SHARING

By considering knowledge ownership and control, the concept of knowledge as a strategic asset begins to emerge. Quintas, Lefrere and Jones (1997) regard knowledge as a key source of advantage for a company. From an industry-competition perspective, once an organization has created a knowledge-based competitive advantage, it becomes much harder for others to compete. The competitive advantage can be protected by maintaining the knowledge advantage. This provides a clear strategic focus for a knowledge-based strategy in contrast to the more general managerial knowledge management concepts. This approach depends on identifying the knowledge content of core competencies, formulating a strategy to disseminate and grow them and building barriers to protect the higher-level types from your competitors. It should also be recognized that, compared to the manufacturing sector it is relatively easy for service sector companies to copy innovations introduced by competitors resulting in a continuous cycle of innovation (Laws, 2004).

Asheima and Coenena (2005) discuss synthetic knowledge where innovation takes place mainly through the application of existing knowledge or through new combinations of knowledge within an industry. This innovation is often incremental and a response to specific problems in the interaction with clients or suppliers and depends on tacit knowledge arising from concrete know-how, craft and practical skills (Asheim & Gertler, 2005).

But to be a strategic asset, knowledge management requires a company-wide policy comprising implementation, monitoring and evaluation. The objective is to ensure that knowledge is available when and where needed, and that it can be acquired from external as well an internal sources. Information and communication technologies (ICT) both ease and speed up the generation and transfer of knowledge within networks. Technology's crucial transformational role is therefore a key part of knowledge management (Gurteen, 1999), and tourism organizations are increasingly dependant on modern information technology.

However, concentration on the technological aspects of knowledge management appears only a small aspect of knowledge sharing. Technology can facilitate sharing but can't create it. Knowledge sharing is instead primarily a socially driven process which can be supported by technology. 'What must come first in the improvement of knowledge production and integration are improvements in the ways people work together to create and to share knowledge' (McElroy, 2003: 58). Knowledge management requires production of knowledge that is useful, transferable to others and of high quality. "It does not mean managing all that is known. It does mean formulating and implementing strategies, improving business processes and monitoring and evaluating what knowledge exists, and its effective management" (Quintas et al., 1997). During the 1990s researchers such as Drucker (1993) and Toffler (1990) recognized that knowledge is a significant resource, and began to analyse its contribution to future power and organisational effectiveness.

KNOWLEDGE AND ORGANIZATIONAL CHANGE

Inkpen (1998: 69) sees new knowledge as providing "the basis for organisational renewal and sustainable competitive advantage." Venzin et al. (1998) distinguished between cognitive and connectionist views of knowledge. In the cognitive perspective, existing knowledge is redefined through new 'incoming' data, information or knowledge. The connectionist view is that the identification of novel relationships and networks leads to new knowledge. This may occur within looser social, or more rigid technical, networks. Knowledge is therefore a product of power relations. Armistead (2002, p. 51) comments that "These discussions resonate with the managerial paradox of improving performance through tight or loose control systems aiming for organisational effectiveness. . . We can interpret this notion further as one of imposition or empowerment. Imposition is associated with bureaucracy, structured systems and attempts to codify all aspects of knowledge. We might expect such perspectives to be more inclined to explicit rather than tacit knowledge. In contrast, empowerment will recognise the potential in the social and individual for knowledge creation and sharing, in which the tacit as much as the explicit aspect of knowledge is engaged."

SHARING KNOWLEDGE IN TOURISM CLUSTERS

A destination is "an amalgam of individual products and experience opportunities that combine to form a total experience of the area visited' (Murphy et al., 2000, 678). As Woods and Deegan note (this volume) this definition underlines how, despite the fragmentation on the supply side, the experience at the destination is perceived as a gestalt by the visitor, and that there is a demand on the part of the consumer for a total quality of experience (QOE) (Otto & Ritchie, 1995). This points to the need for effective knowledge sharing in destinations.

Many studies of industrial clusters imply that all firms in a geographic area perform similarly, but (Tallman & Jenkins, 2002) comment that even casual observation must raise questions about this idea. Their analysis shows that the success of some geographic clusters seems to be tied to the interaction of member firms that evolved in some loosely defined manner, but without prior planning. It may be that alternative groupings built around similar strategies (Peteraf & Shanley, 1997) or alliance relationships (Gomes-Casseres, 1994) might show the same collective performance for firms without geographical ties. This hierarchy of specialized knowledge stocks at both firm and cluster levels, and the specificity of knowledge resources at each level is protected, in part, by asymmetries in knowledge flows from level to level. These asymmetries result from organization-specific architectural under-standings of the industry embedded in the social milieu of the cluster" Tallman et al. (Tallman & Jenkins, 2002).

They examine advantage-generating "superfirm" groups inside industries, "within which member firms simultaneously share and differentiate sources of competitive advantage. For competitive advantage to function at a cluster level, knowledge must be shared among the firms in the regional cluster, yet for competitive advantage to exist at the firm level, at least some knowledge must remain private. Component knowledge provides competitive advantage to the originating firm so long as it remains in private hands (Matusik & Hill, 1998), retaining its unique, valuable, rent-earning capacity within the firm" (Barney, 1991; Tallman & Jenkins, 2002).

Knowledge transfer with external partners is also important. Strategic partnerships provide mutual access to other companies' knowledge.

Research and training agreements with universities and other research institutions provide companies with access to recent research knowledge. Cooke et al., (1998) argued that a regional innovation system is in place under two conditions. The regional production structure consists of firms displaying clustering tendencies, and there is a regional supportive infrastructure or knowledge generation subsystem such as public and private research laboratories, universities and colleges, technology transfer agencies, and vocational training organisations. This constitutes systems of innovation (Edquist, 1997), interaction networks (Kaufmann and Todtling, 2001).

COMMUNITIES OF PRACTICE

Coakes (Coakes, 2004) refers to Communities of Practice (CoPs). "CoPs are becoming the core knowledge strategy for global organizations. Communities of practice are held together by a common interest in a body of knowledge and are driven by a desire and need to share problems, experiences, insights, templates, tools, and best practices. CoPs channel knowledge flow and promote consistent and standardized knowledge sharing throughout an organization. These communities give organizations the structures and processes needed to quickly identify and exchange valuable knowledge capital to drive business results" (APQC, 2004a). Woods and Deegan (this issue), note that three elements define a community of practice; domain, community and practice. A knowledge domain is a topic that people share an interest in and knowledge of. People organise around a domain of knowledge that gives members a sense of joint enterprise and brings them together. Members identify with the domain of knowledge and a joint undertaking that emerges from a shared understanding of their situation. The second element, community, describes relationships of mutual engagement that bind members together in a social entity. A community interacts regularly and engages in joint activities that build relationships and trust. A community refers to 'who they are' and how they function together. Finally, a community does something and this is 'practice.' The community builds capability in practice by developing shared repertoires and resources (tools, documents, routines, vocabulary, symbols, artifacts, etc.) that embody the accumulated knowledge of the community. This accumulated knowledge serves as a foundation for future learning (Wenger, McDermott and Snyder, 2002). In CoPs the geographic proximity of participants is less significant than their shared motivations.

CoPs foster individual professional development as well as organisational learning. Vestal [2003] describes four ways in which they operate, innovation, problem solving, sharing best practice, stewarding (organizing) knowledge across the CoP. One example presented in this issue is by Hawkins who has described the knowledge-roles of networks of academic institutions in tourism. He regards it as the responsibility of higher education institutions to transfer knowledge to the governmental, commercial and civil society components of the tourism sector.

STRUCTURE OF THIS VOLUME

The papers in this special issue examine these issues within a variety of contexts. Hawkins emphasizes the responsibility of higher education institutions to transfer knowledge to the governmental, commercial and civil society components of the tourism and hospitality sector, which he defines in operational terms as transferring knowledge into practice through research, teaching, and service. He analyzes the benefits of a comprehensive networking approach, and discusses the example of the CRC in Australia. STRC's mission is the development and management of intellectual property (IP) to deliver innovation to business, community and government enhancing the environmental, economic and social sustainability of tourism.

The paper by Pearce and Benckendorff examines benchmarking in the attractions sector of tourism as an example of sharing of knowledge. Here knowledge is operational and geared to improving the performance of existing operators. It examines the characteristics of tourism and why operators have made little use of benchmarking emphasising difficulties in sharing of knowledge such as government sensitivity, difficulty in defining and resourcing research and competitive concerns. They note that knowledge is power.

Woods and Deegan discuss the formation of a group of operators—formally a community of practice based around the formation of a quality brand. This brand was ineffective in its original purpose but was effective in creating trust and sharing of information. This was considered in part due to operators knowing each other. It was also encouraged by particular people. Knowledge management was seen as a social process. Clark and Scott examines knowledge sharing and management within a State Tourism Office. This paper examines the development of strategy as a function of knowledge sharing. Here knowledge management is seen as 'a process, that integrates people, technology and organisational processes in the course of organising, refining and distributing knowledge throughout the organization.' They conclude that creation of successful knowledge management as embodied by a strategic plan is dependent on a culture of knowledge sharing. Zehrer and Pechlaner examine the importance of creating and sharing relevant knowledge in a destination employing mystery shopping as a tool to test its effectiveness. Here the reflexivity and importance of people both in the creation of quality and production knowledge as well as in the use of that knowledge is interwoven with the theme of ownership and trust of employees. Pan, Scott and Laws discuss the different perspectives involved in identifying knowledge gaps and the complexity in sharing knowledge across different organizations using the recent experience of catering to Chinese inbound tourists to test the effectiveness of knowledge sharing within the Australian tourism sector.

The special issue concludes with two case studies. Lemelin discusses the development of a system for sharing knowledge that illustrates the importance of understanding the interorganizational relationships and complexity in sharing knowledge as well as presenting a 'best practice' model for sharing knowledge that balances the needs of all parties involved.

CONCLUSION

Clearly, knowledge sharing is a means by which new ideas and competitive advantage is created or brought into an organization (destination or network) and incorporated into new ways of functioning. This introductory discussion and the papers in this volume emphasise the social aspects of knowledge sharing as well as the more well researched managerial aspects of knowledge systems. Knowledge sharing raises issues of power and control, of who the knowledge is being used by as much as what the knowledge is. This creates tensions between the individual and the organization in the release of tacit knowledge and focuses attention on the difficulty of sharing knowledge in tourism destinations where operators both compete and cooperate.

The papers in this special issue have provides some directions for future research avenues. One area for research is knowledge sharing in different contexts as a lens to understand power within the tourism system. This involves examining questions like: "How can tacit knowledge best be localised?" and "How can tacit knowledge be kept within a company?" A further research focus of increasing interest is the insight to be gained into the operation of tourism by using knowledge theory as a lens to examine, firstly organizational functioning and change issues, and secondly the ways in which the industry clusters and networks both at operational levels and at the scale of destinations.

From a more positivist perspective, improvement in knowledge transfer would appear to hold great promise for tourism destinations and indeed tourism provides a useful context for such research. Tourism destinations involve different cultural environments and often less cohesive goals than other types of organization. Finally, while there has been much discussion of the potential for knowledge management and sharing, research on if, and how, it works would be useful.

REFERENCES

Armistead, C., & Meakins, M. (2002). A framework for practising knowledge management. *Long Range Planning, 35*(1), 49-71.

Asheim, B. T., & Coenen, L. (2005). Knowledge bases and regional innovation systems: Comparing Nordic clusters. *Research Policy, 34,* 1173–1190.

Asheim, B. T., & Gertler, M. S. (2005). The geography of innovation: regional innovation systems. In J. Fagerberg, D. Mowery & R. Nelson (Eds.), *The Oxford Handbook of Innovation* (pp. 291-317). Oxford: Oxford University Press.

Buckley, P. J., & Carter, M. J. (2002). Process and Structure in Knowledge Management Practices of British and US Multinational Enterprises. *Journal of International Management, 8*(1), 29-48.

Coakes, E. (2004). Knowledge management: A Primer. *Communications of the Association for Information Systems, 14,* 406-489.

Cooper, C. (2002). Knowledge Management and Research Commercialisation Agendas. *Current Issues in Tourism, 5*(5), 375-377.

Cooper, C. (2005). *Managing Tourism Knowledge: Concepts and Approaches.* London: Channel View.

Drucker, P. (1993). *Post Capitalist Society.* New York: Harper Business.

Drucker, P. (1999). Knowledge-worker productivity: The biggest challenge. *California Management Review, 41,* 79-94.

Fischer, M. M., & Frohlich, J. (2001). Knowledge, Complexity and Innovation Systems: Prologue. In J. Frohlich (Ed.), *Knowledge, Complexity and Innovation Systems* (pp. 1-17). Heidelberg: Springer.

Gates, B., & Hemmingway, C. (1999). *Business @ the Speed of Thought.* New York: Warner Books Inc.

Gurteen, D. (1999). Creating a knowledge sharing culture. *Knowledge Management, 2*(5), 24-27.

Harris, D. B. (1996). *Creating a Knowledge Centric Information Technology Environment,* from http://www.dbharris.com/ckc.htm

Inkpen, A. C. (1998). Learning and Knowledge Acquisition Through International Strategic Alliances. *The Academy of Management Executive*, *12*(4), 69-80.

Jafari, J. (1990). Research and scholarship: The basis of tourism education. *Journal of Tourism Studies*, *1*(1), 33-41.

Jordon, J., & Jones, P. (1997). Assessing your Company's Knowledge Management Style. *Long Range Planning*, *30*(3), 392-398.

Laws, E. (2004). Improving Tourism and Hospitality Services. CAB International, Oxford.

Kodama, M. (2005). Knowledge Creation through Networked Strategic Communities: Case Studies on New Product Development in Japanese Companies. *Long Range Planning*, *38*, 27-49.

Marshall, A. (1890). *Principles of Economics*. London: MacMillan.

McElroy, M. W. (2003). *The New Knowledge Management Complexity: Learning and Sustainable Innovation*. London: Butterworth-Heinemann.

Michael, E. J. (2003). Tourism micro-clusters. *Tourism Economics*, *9*(2), 133–145.

Murphy, P., Pritchard, M. P., & Smith, B. (2000). The destination product and its impact on traveller perceptions. *Tourism Management*, *21*, 43-52.

Nonaka, I., Reinmoeller, P., & Senoo, D. (1998). The 'ART' of Knowledge: Systems to Capitalize on Market Knowledge. *European Management Journal*, *16*(6), 673-684.

Nonaka, I., & Takeuchi, H. (1995). *The Knowledge-Creating Company: How Japanese Companies Create the Dynamics of Innovation*. Oxford: Oxford University Press.

Nonaka, I., Toyama, R., & Konno, N. (2000). SECI, Ba and leadership: a unified model of dynamic knowledge Creation. *Long Range Planning*, *33*, 5-34.

Otto, J. E., & Ritchie, J. R. B. (1995). Exploring the Quality of the Service Experience: A Theoretical and Empirical Analysis. *Advances in Services Marketing and Management*, *5*, 37-63.

Pechlaner, H., Abfalter, D., & Raich, F. (2002). Cross-Border Destination Management Systems in the Alpine Region-The Role of Knowledge Networks on the Example of AlpNet. *Journal of Quality Assurance in Hospitality & Tourism*, *3*(3/4), 89-107.

Polanyi, M. (1958). *Personal Knowledge: Towards a Post-critical Philosophy*. Oxford: University of Chicago Press.

Quintas, P., Lefrere, P., & Jones, J. (1997). Knowledge management: A strategic agenda. *Long Range Planning*, *30*(3), 385-391.

Saxena, G. (2005). Relationships, networks and the learning regions: case evidence from the Peak District National Park. *Tourism Management*, *26*, 277-289.

Schlegelmilch, B. B., & Penz, E. (2002). Knowledge Management in Marketing. *The Marketing Review*, *3*(1), 5-19.

Shin, M., Holden, T., & Schmidt, R. A. (2001). From Knowledge Theory to Management Practice: Towards an Integrated Approach. *Information Processing & Management*, *37*(2), 335-355.

Tallman, S., & Jenkins, M. (2002). Alliances, knowledge flows, and performance in regional clusters. In F. J. Contractor & P. Lorange (Eds.), *Cooperative Strategies and Alliances* (pp. 203-216). London: Pergamon.

Toffler, A. (1990). *Powershift*. New York: Bantam.

Venzin, M., von Krogh, G., & Roos, J. (1998). Future Research into Knowledge Management. In G. von Krogh, J. Roos & D. Kleine (Eds.), *Knowing in Firms. Understanding, Managing and Measuring Knowledge*. New York: Sage.

Whitehill, M. (1997). Knowledge-based strategy to deliver sustained competitive advantage. *Long Range Planning, 30*(4), 621-627.

Willke, H. (1998). *Systemisches Wissensmanagement*. Stuttgart: Lucius & Lucius.

Zack, M. H. (1999a). Developing a Knowledge Strategy. *California Management Review, 41*(3), 125-145.

Zack, M. H. (1999b). Managing Codified Knowledge. *Sloan Management Review, 40*(4), 45-58.

doi:10.1300/J162v07n01_01

Transferring Tourism Knowledge: The Role of Higher Education Institutions

Donald E. Hawkins

SUMMARY. Knowledge sharing and quality assurance in hospitality and tourism is a very broad topic to cover. This paper focuses mainly on the role of higher education in transferring knowledge into practice. Knowledge can be defined as "an understanding of something and the ability to use that understanding through study and experience."[1] doi:10.1300/J162v07n01_02 *[Article copies available for a fee from The Haworth Document Delivery Service: 1-800-HAWORTH. E-mail address: <docdelivery@haworthpress.com> Website: <http://www.HaworthPress.com> © 2006 by The Haworth Press, Inc. All rights reserved.]*

KEYWORDS. Knowledge sharing, universities, tourism

Donald E. Hawkins is Eisenhower Professor of Tourism Policy, School of Business and Public Management, George Washington University, Washington, DC (E-mail: dhawk@gwu.edu).

An earlier version of this paper was presented at TOURCOM Conference organized by the World Tourism Organization, Madrid, January 28-30, 2004, and then published in Observations on International Tourism Communications, Conference Report from the First World Conference on Tourism Communications, 29-30 January 2004, Madrid, Spain, May 2004 by WTO, pp. 107-119.

[Haworth co-indexing entry note]: "Transferring Tourism Knowledge: The Role of Higher Education Institutions." Hawkins, Donald E. Co-published simultaneously in *Journal of Quality Assurance in Hospitality & Tourism* (The Haworth Hospitality Press, an imprint of The Haworth Press, Inc.) Vol. 7, No. 1/2, 2006, pp. 13-27; and: *Knowledge Sharing and Quality Assurance in Hospitality and Tourism* (ed: Noel Scott and Eric Laws) The Haworth Hospitality Press, an imprint of The Haworth Press, Inc., 2006, pp. 13-27. Single or multiple copies of this article are available for a fee from The Haworth Document Delivery Service [1-800-HAWORTH. 9:00 a.m. - 5:00 p.m. (EST). E-mail address: docdelivery@haworthpress.com].

Available online at http://jqaht.haworthpress.com
© 2006 by The Haworth Press, Inc. All rights reserved.
doi:10.1300/J162v07n01_02

KNOWLEDGE TRANSFER NETWORKING APPROACH

As the Chairman of the WTO Education Council, George Washington University has proposed that that our members adopt a comprehensive networking approach emphasizing the responsibility of higher education institutions to transfer knowledge to the governmental, commercial and civil society components of the tourism and hospitality sector.

According to the American Productivity and Quality Center (APQC), knowledge transfer is a cyclical process. The ultimate goal of knowledge transfer is knowledge use. As obvious as that may seem, many organizations have little idea if the knowledge they attempt to share is actually being used.

APQC recommends that networks be formed "to study how outstanding organizations design and deploy successful approaches to identify, capture, and share information and knowledge so that use and reuse are optimized. The ability to rapidly identify and transfer superior practices is an important source of competitive advantage. As the economy grows, transfer and reuse will be the fastest way to grow without adding undue costs. No matter the industry, reusing successfully demonstrated practices can lead to shorter cycle times, faster ramp-up, higher customer satisfaction, better decisions, and lower costs."[2] The knowledge transfer process describes the creation of knowledge and its transfer though identification, collection, review, sharing, adaptation, adoption steps leading to its use.

As stated earlier, using and reusing accepted practices can lead to the improvement of organizational effectiveness. Scientific, professional and trade networks in the tourism sector have given increasing importance to benchmarking to improve the performance of organizations, employing processes similar to the APQC approach described above.

Wober[3] describes internal and external benchmarking approaches. Internal refers to the functions and activities of an organization at the same or different locations. External benchmarking involves the use of (a) best practices regardless of sector/industry or to improve performance and learn from others; (b) comparative analysis of performance objectives, strategies, and activities of competitors in a sector/industry to improve competitiveness; and (c) policies, strategies, information systems, training programs designed to improve a sector/industry. Wober classifies benchmarking in tourism to encompass profit-oriented firms, nonprofit organizations and destinations. Most of the benchmarking initiatives have been focused on profit-making firms, particularly in the hospitality industry. Few initiatives have been undertaken for non-profit or destination organizations.

HIGHER EDUCATION'S ROLE
IN KNOWLEDGE MANAGEMENT

Higher education institutions have begun to recognize that they play an increasingly important role in knowledge management (KM). As Hallal has stated: "In an age when knowledge has surpassed capital as the strategic factor driving the global economy, KM deserves some portion of the enormous effort now expended on accounting, financial analysis, capital investment and the vast infrastructure devoted to sheer money."[4]

Throughout history, higher education institutions have been challenged to both create and disseminate knowledge. Often, our efforts have been characterized as an "ivory tower" approach not related to practical realties. Today, higher education's role, in my judgment, should be to facilitate KM, which can be operationally defined as transferring knowledge into practice through research, teaching, and service, as described in Figure 1.[5]

Teaching, research, and service scholarship can lead to the transfer of knowledge to practice through the functions of discovery, integration, application, and education, as described below:

Discovery of Knowledge. Discovery involves being the first to find out, to know, or to reveal original or revised theories, principles, knowledge, or creations. Academic discovery reflects "the commitment to knowledge for its own sake, to freedom of inquiry and to following, in a disciplined fashion, an investigation wherever it may lead."[6] Discovery includes identifying new or revised theoretical principles and models, insights about how empirical phenomena operate, and original creations in literature, performance, or production in the arts, architecture, design, video, and broadcast media.

Integration of Knowledge. Integration involves "making connections across the disciplines, placing the specialties in larger context, illuminating data in a revealing way, often educating non specialists, too." Integration creates new knowledge by bringing together otherwise isolated knowledge from two or more disciplines or fields thus creating new insights and understanding. It is "serious, disciplined work that seeks to interpret, draw together and bring new insight to bear on original re-

FIGURE 1. Transferring Knowledge into Practice

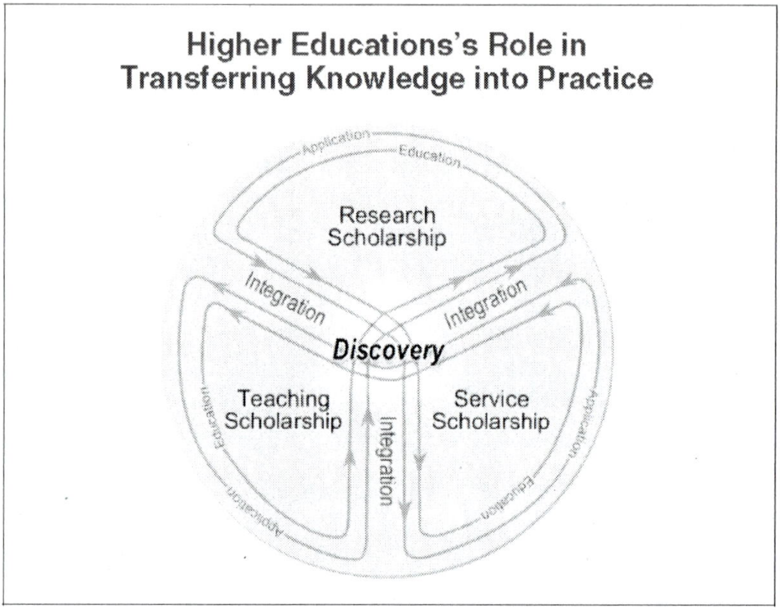

search." It means "interpretation, fitting one's own research–or the research of others–into larger intellectual patterns."[7] Integration brings divergent knowledge, artistic creations, or original works together. Integration may occur within or between teaching, research, and service scholarship.

Application of Knowledge. Application involves bringing knowledge to bear in addressing significant societal issues. It engages the scholar in asking, "How can knowledge be responsibly applied to consequential problems? How can it be helpful to individuals as well as institutions?"[8] Application involves the use of knowledge or reactive activities for development and change. With the first two functions, scholars define the topics for inquiry. With application, groups, organizations, community, government, or emergent societal issues define the agenda for scholarship.

Education. Education involves developing the knowledge, skill, mind, character, or ability of others. It "means not only transmitting knowledge, but transforming and extending it as well." Education stimulates "active, not passive, learning and encourages students to be critical, creative thinkers, with the capacity to go on learning. . . . It is a dynamic endeavor involving all the analogies, metaphors, and images that build bridges between the teacher's understanding and the student's learning. Pedagogical procedures must be carefully planned, continuously examined, and relate directly to the subject taught."[9]

NETWORKING THROUGH OUTREACH STRATEGIES

Outreach is a networking concept that describes a wide range of activities that involve universities can employ to create, identify, collect, review, share, and adopt/adapt knowledge leading to its use in practice. Outreach is not synonymous with "service" nor is it limited to cooperative extension and continuing education. Rather, outreach should be inherent in teaching, research, and service–i.e.,

> *Outreach research* includes a wide spectrum of cooperative discovery, application, and creative problem-solving interactions between the university and external audiences. It includes policy and applied research, technology transfer partnerships, demonstration projects, creative works in the arts, and related interactions between university scholars and external audiences to discover, explore, and disseminate knowledge in practice.
>
> *Outreach teaching* includes instruction and interpretation through cooperative extension and continuing education. Presentations to nonacademic and professional audiences, the World Campus, and other extensions of instruction to benefit society are also outreach teaching.
>
> *Outreach service* involves faculty sharing their expertise with a variety of audiences including service to the various professional and learned societies, participation in community affairs as a representative of the university, and service to communities, governments, and corporations. It includes clinical service delivery, participation in task forces, authorities, public hearings, professional performances, and other venues based on the expertise of faculty members.[10]

The examples which follow demonstrate outreaching networking approaches involving universities and the tourism sector.

OUTREACH RESEARCH EXAMPLE:
SUSTAINABLE TOURISM CRC (STCRC)

The Sustainable Tourism CRC (STCRC) was established under the Australian Government's Cooperative Research Centers Program to underpin the development of a dynamic, internationally competitive, and sustainable tourism industry. The STCRC is a not-for-profit company owned by its industry, government and university partners.

STRC's vision is innovation driving a dynamic, internationally competitive and sustainable tourism industry. STRC's mission is the development and management of intellectual property (IP) to deliver innovation to business, community and government enhancing the environmental, economic and social sustainability of tourism–one of the world's largest, fastest growing industries.

Destination Australia is STCRC's integrated, multidisciplinary research program, focusing on three key areas:

- Sustainable Destinations
- Sustainable Enterprises
- Sustainable Resources

STCRC diffuses its research outputs to industry through:

- Collaboration with industry and government partners
- Spin-off enterprises
- Licensing its intellectual property
- Business tools, kits, manuals and expert systems
- Conferences, workshops, seminars
- Published reports, fact sheets and extension flyers
- Internet-based information services
- Training products, courses and programs
- International consulting services.

Recent accomplishments of the Sustainable Tourism CRC include the following:

1. Bringing tourism into the major Australia Government research and development initiative–the Cooperative Research Centers program
2. Strengthening collaborative links between industry, tourism research organizations, educational institutions and government agencies

3. Funding post graduate sustainable tourism research issues
4. Focusing the collective export potential of Australia's leading tertiary level tourism, travel and hospitality providers
5. Assisting the industry understand and value the benefit of a research based, strategic knowledge approach to addressing complex tourism issues
6. Assisting the Australian Government's decision to (a) re-join WTO (b) take an active role in the establishment and development of the APEC Tourism Working Group (c) establishing and hosting the APEC International Centre for Sustainable Tourism AICST
7. Establishing or supporting spin-off companies to take the intellectual property generated from CRC research to the marketplace
8. Leading the Australian/South Pacific research into WTO's ST–EP Program
9. Providing Australian focus for the following tourism research agenda:

   - Tourism environmental management research (Wildlife Tourism, Mountain Tourism, Nature Tourism, Adventure Tourism)
   - Tourism engineering design & eco-technology research (Coastal and marine infrastructure and systems, coastal tourism ecology, Waste management, water supply and associated environmental impact studies, Physical infrastructure, design and construction)
   - Tourism policy, products and business research (Consumers and marketing, Events & sports tourism, Strategic management, business planning, and development, Destination management and regional tourism, Tourism economics and policy, Indigenous tourism)
   - E-travel and tourism research (Electronic product and destination marketing & selling, IT for travel and tourism online development, Rural & regional tourism online development, E-business innovation in sustainable travel and tourism)
   - Tourism education

10. The CRC has also established dedicated research centers at partner Universities:

    - Centre for Regional Tourism Research at Southern Cross University
    - Centre for Tourism Risk Management, University of Queensland

- Qantas Chair in Tourism Economics, U. of New South Wales

11. Publications: a large volume of high quality research generated by the CRC's projects can be viewed on the CRC website publications catalogue
12. Providing research and operational horse-power and support to Green Globe throughout the world.[11]

STCRC is developing Australia's long-term tourism research capacities through a vigorous postgraduate research education program, supported by scholarships for students in industry-designed projects, and by developing and distributing education and training products.

The Cooperative Research Centers Program is a major research and development initiative of the Australian Government. This program was established to boost the competitiveness of Australia by strengthening in collaborative links between industry, research organizations, educational institutions and relevant government agencies. It aims to bring the highest quality research providers and industry together to focus on outcomes for businesses and communities.[12]

OUTREACH TEACHING EXAMPLE:
E-LEARNING COOPERATION MODEL

Distance learning, online education, e-learning and other terms have surfaced in the last decade to describe a variety of approaches to using the Internet and other information technologies to enable instructors in one place to deliver learning experiences to students located in other places, sometimes continents away.

The field has grown dramatically because e-learning offers a number of higher education advantages for certain student populations over the traditional single-site classroom approach, such as[13]

1. Student-centered learning rather than faculty-centered instruction
2. Writing intensity that improves written expression
3. Highly interactive discussions involving all students rather than just extraverts
4. More closely geared to interests of lifelong learners
5. Rapid feedback to questions and submitted assignments
6. Learning flexibility in a time-deficient world

7. A more intimate community of learners
8. Expanded learning opportunities for those tied to their residences.

Two institutions of higher education with TedQual-certified programs–the Université du Québec à Montréal (UQAM) and The George Washington University (GWU)–have developed an E-learning Cooperation Model to enhance the delivery of tourism education in developing countries. This development was stimulated by the opportunities provided by the Memorandum of Understanding on Cooperation signed in 1999 between The World Tourism Organization (WTO) and The World Bank Group.

The Model is based on the project proposal entitled "Information Technology (IT) Strategy for Tourism Education in Africa–a Joint Initiative of the WTO and the World Bank Group" which received the support from the WTO Commission for Africa during its XXXVII Assembly, Seoul, Republic of Korea, 24 September 2001. While we focus on Africa in this elaboration of the Model here, it may be applied to any developing regions in the world.

Figure 2 summarizes the E-learning Cooperation Model, which begins with:

- Digitalizing contents of all existing WTO GTAT courses for delivery online or on CD-ROM; and
- Adapting digitalized program contents from participating TedQual-certified institutions, and developing new content where needed. For example, the GWU Accelerated Master of Tourism Administration (AMTA) graduate degree program, which meets TedQual standards, offers a bank of 15 courses now delivered online. Graduate courses from other TedQual certified institutions might be incorporated in the curriculum options, as well. UQAM can assist the translation of such courses into the French language and add content directly relevant to Francophone countries in Africa.

We anticipate that implementing this Model will produce the following constructive outcomes:

- At least one group from the GTAT series of seminars and courses, which contents have been digitalized and offered to tourism managers in public and private sector workplaces, will be presented in each of the WTO member states in Africa;

- At least one university from each of the WTO member states in Africa will present a high quality program in management of tourism, employing IT tools for tourism education;
- At least one university from each of the WTO member states in Africa will apply for TedQual certification. GWU and UQAM, in collaboration with other interested TedQual-certified institutions, will offer capacity-building activities and direct mentoring to these TedQual candidates.

We are also exploring the ways and means by which this model might also be developed for the Indian Ocean and other regions of the World. The WTO Education Council is currently surveying its members to determine their distance learning capabilities and interest in joining this network. For example, George Washington University through its Blackboard E-Learning platform offers an extensive series of continuing education unit (CEU) courses that lead to a Tourism Destination

FIGURE 2. E-Learning Cooperation Model

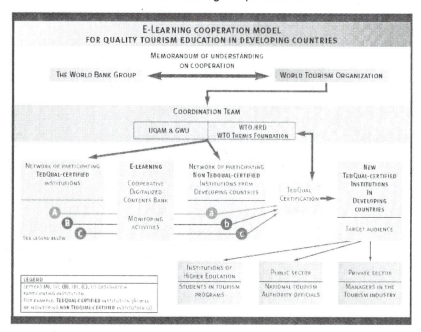

Source: Bédard, Hawkins, and Frechtling (2004)

Management and Marketing Certificate and an Event Management Certificate. With development assistance funding, we have offered courses delivered through customized workshops enhanced by distance education learning for a tour operator certificate in Jordan, and a Sales Academy course for the International Association of Visitor and Convention Bureaus.[14]

OUTREACH SERVICE EXAMPLE: DEVELOPMENT ASSISTANCE NETWORK FOR TOURISM ENHANCEMENT AND INVESTMENT (DANTEI)

As one of the largest global industries and employers, tourism has a significant role in the economies of both developed and developing countries. According to the World Bank's "World Development Indicators" 2002 report, more than 70% of the world's poorest countries are reliant on tourism as a key economic growth engine. Acknowledging this, development assistance projects are increasingly using tourism as a means of fostering sustainable development. However, there is a paucity of information concerning appropriate engagement levels and policy guidance for development assistance in efforts to enhance tourism revenues for developing economies. There are difficulties in balancing the public sector role while maintaining a competitive private sector environment; also in balancing community needs and dealing with social issues Development assistance for tourism only really has a history of 20-30 years, and in most countries, sustainable tourism is an ongoing social, economic and environmental process of trail and error.

In 2001 George Washington University's International Institute of Tourism Studies (GWU/IITS) began a project to populate a database of world-wide donor funded tourism projects. The incentive for this initiative was the absence of consistent information about the sources or benefits of tourism projects in developing countries, and the missed opportunity to learn from experiences that would undoubtedly be of value to all stakeholders. During the past two years of research by GW's IITS, 363 ongoing projects, from over 20 different donors, with a total value of more than US$9.43 billion estimated for period 2001-10, have been identified; refer to Table 1 for further details.

Internet access to this database and the process of learning from it and utilizing it as a development tool, are the foundations of the DANTEI initiative. DANTEI, as an interactive resource base, offers a range of

TABLE 1. Development Assistance Funding Estimates 2001-2010

Region	Funding (US $ Billions)	Number of Projects
Asia and Near East	3.58	89
Latin America and Caribbean	1.58	138
Africa	.65	89
Europe and Eurasia	3.62	47
Total	9.43	363

benefits to tourism developers, stakeholders and donors as well as a credible platform for knowledge exchange and international co-operation. Donors are unified in support of the Millennium Development Goals (MDGs) and improved knowledge management and international cooperation are key elements in the strategy for achieving the MDGs. DANTEI offers an opportunity, in a highly visible sector, to promote and deliver improved collaboration, knowledge management and the promotion of sustainable tourism practices.

DANTEI aims to become a leading global partnership that promotes sustainable tourism initiatives with development assistance resources. It will achieve this by facilitating information exchange, knowledge applications (tools, practices, case studies, models and lessons learned), training programs and co-operation and understanding between the private sector, governments and civil society. DANTEI will anchor this knowledge management system with core values of transparency, collaboration, accuracy, user-friendly accessibility and shared responsibility.

The development of sustainable tourism involves diverse stakeholders who all have significant roles and information requirements at different times. These stakeholders tend to have well-defined parameters within which they communicate and operate. In order to build partnerships and create genuine knowledge sharing between these stakeholders, the operational characteristics and information pathways of each stakeholder group need to be understood and facilitated to interface with DANTEI and thereby each other (Figure 3).

DANTEI design activities focus on the cluster groups represented in this schematic diagram. It is expected that primary relationships for DANTEI will be established with the stakeholders represented by the darker circles, with particular emphasis on donor policies and practices.

FIGURE 3. DANTEI Stakeholders

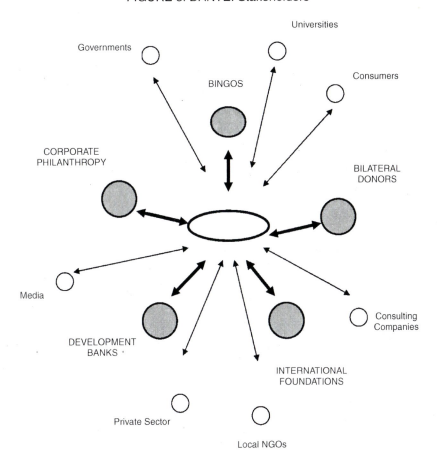

The outer ring of stakeholders represents the ultimate user beneficiaries of DANTEI. seeks to establish an on-going dialogue between developing country needs and donor policies related tourism development. To assist with this formidable task, DANTEI is in the process of creating regional centers in the Asia Pacific region in cooperation with the University of Hawaii's School of Travel Industry Management and in Europe with key collaborators.

Community of Practice. GWU/IITS has also catalyzed the process of creating a "Community of Practice" network of professional staff with expertise in sustainable tourism from donor agencies in North

America and is encouraging a similar development through networks in Europe and Asia. These virtual communities will help guide and promote awareness of DANTEI in donor agencies in the coming months and contribute to the content of DANTEI in the future. UNCTAD has agreed to facilitate information exchange under their Sustainable Tourism for Development collaborative initiative: http://tourism.unctad. org/QuickPlace/sustainable-tourism-for-development/Main.nsf/h_Toc/ E972857E85B32490C1256D4B00299FA2/?OpenDocument.

Internet Platform–One of the key activities towards the development of DANTEI was the Tourism Policy Forum, conducted by the World Tourism Organization in Washington, D.C. on October 18-20, 2004. At the Forum, the internet platform was launched in collaboration with WTO. For full details, go to www.dantei.org

Post-forum work on DANTEI will incorporate case studies and will focus on positioning DANTEI as the leading sustainable tourism Internet portal. It is envisaged that DANTEI will become a focal point for best practices and development assistance guidelines.

Delivering Training Through DANTEI–The DANTEI network will provide an opportunity to deliver targeted and meaningful training to a range of potential user groups. During the market research period of development, training needs were identified and courses formulated to meet these needs. There is potential for DANTEI to work with other partners at a local level to deliver training with a priority emphasis on identifying and accessing funding from foundations, corporate philanthropy, and multilateral/bi-lateral donors. This would be a cost effective way to reach grass roots tourism entrepreneurs (such as community based tourism businesses), destination management organizations, higher education institutions, NGOs and protected area managers in developing countries.

CONCLUSION

Higher education institutions have a critical role to play in transferring knowledge into practice. This paper provides a rationale for colleges, universities and other training institutions to facilitate knowledge though outreach activities involving research, teaching and service. Three practical examples are provided to illustrate an outreach approach. On going partnerships between higher education institutions and the tourism sector at all levels are needed to transfer knowledge into practical use.

NOTES

1. The Newbury House Dictionary of American English, Monroe Allen Publishers, 2000, p. 479

2. APQC is a pioneer in knowledge management (KM). Based on the experiences of more than 350 organizations implementing KM, APQC has captured the best practices and created a proven methodology: APQC's Road Map to KnowledgeManagement Results: Stages of Implementation™. Since its 1995 knowledge management symposium, APQC has conducted 14 KM-specific consortium benchmarking studies. For details, go to: http://www.apqc.org

3. Wober, Karl W., Benchmarking in Tourism and Hospitality Industries, CABI, 2002, p. 3

4. Halal, William E., The Logic of Knowledge: How a Knowledge Economy Differs from a Capital Economy, unpublished paper, George Washington University, Washington, DC, p.2.

5. Unified Knowledge System Concept for Overall Performance Evaluation, Pennsylvania State University, 2001.http://keystone21.cas.psu.edu/uniscope/

6. Boyer, Ernest L., *Scholarship Reconsidered: Priorities of the Professorate*, The Carnegie Foundation for the Advancement of Teaching, 1990, p17.

7. Boyer, op. cit. pp18-19.

8. Ibid, p22.

9. Ibid, pp23-24.

10. Unified Knowledge System Concept for Overall Performance Evaluation, Pennsylvania State University, February 2001. http:/keystone21.cas.psu.edu/uniscope.

11. Correspondence from Steve Noakes, General Manager, STCRC, January 2004.

12. Source and for further details, go to http://www.crctourism.com.au/

13. Adapted from Mark Kassop "Ten Ways Online Education Matches, or Surpasses, Face-to-Face Learning." The Technology Source, May/June 2003. (Available online athttp://ts.mivu.org/default.asp?show=article&id=1059).

14. For complete information on these programs, please go to www.gwutourism. org.

REFERENCES

Boyer, Ernest L., *Scholarship Reconsidered: Priorities of the Professorate*, The Carnegie Foundation for the Advancement of Teaching, 1990.

Bedard, F. and Hawkins, D. and Frechtling, D. "E-Learning Cooperation Model for Tourism Education in Developing Countries," *Tourism's Potential as a Sustainable Development Strategy*, Madrid, Spain, World Tourism Organization, 2004. pp. 77-81.

Halal, William E., The Logic of Knowledge: How a Knowledge Economy Differs from a Capital Economy, unpublished paper, George Washington University, Washington, DC.

Ruhanen, L and Cooper, C., *Developing a Knowledge Management Approach to Tourism Research*, TedQual, No. 6, 1/2003. WTO.Themis Publication.

Wober, Karl W., Benchmarking in Tourism and Hospitality Industries, CABI, 2002.

doi:10.1300/J162v07n01_02

Benchmarking, Usable Knowledge and Tourist Attractions

Philip Pearce
Pierre Benckendorff

SUMMARY. The article considers the special needs of the attractions sector for comparative and comprehensive information on parallel operations. It defines and articulates four kinds of benchmarking and explores the potential of this empirical approach to knowledge acquisition. Some comparisons and a synthesis of benchmarking studies from the hotel sector, from tour operators and from the national park management world are included in the conceptual appraisal of the benchmarking approach. The study seeks to apply and illustrate the benchmarking approach to tourist attractions. A large scale survey study of Australian tourist attractions considers the value of 15 indicators and illustrates how they provide contrasts among different kinds of attractions. The research presented also provides examples of easy access graphical information as an illustration of research findings and acts as an exemplar of the knowledge communication process. Important distinctions are drawn between knowledge generated by analysts and knowledge fitting the needs of managers. doi:10.1300/J162v07n01_03 *[Article copies available for a fee from The Haworth Document Delivery Service: 1-800-HAWORTH. E-mail address: <docdelivery@haworthpress.com> Website: <http://www.HaworthPress.com> © 2006 by The Haworth Press, Inc. All rights reserved.]*

Philip Pearce (E-mail: Philip.Pearce@jcu.edu.au) is Professor of Tourism and Pierre Benckendorff (E-mail: Pierre.Benckendorff@jcu.edu.au) is Lecturer, School of Business, James Cook University, Townsville, Queensland 4811, Australia.

[Haworth co-indexing entry note]: "Benchmarking, Usable Knowledge and Tourist Attractions." Pearce, Philip, and Pierre Benckendorff. Co-published simultaneously in *Journal of Quality Assurance in Hospitality & Tourism* (The Haworth Hospitality Press, an imprint of The Haworth Press, Inc.) Vol. 7, No. 1/2, 2006, pp. 29-52; and: *Knowledge Sharing and Quality Assurance in Hospitality and Tourism* (ed: Noel Scott and Eric Laws) The Haworth Hospitality Press, an imprint of The Haworth Press, Inc., 2006, pp. 29-52. Single or multiple copies of this article are available for a fee from The Haworth Document Delivery Service [1-800-HAWORTH, 9:00 a.m. - 5:00 p.m. (EST). E-mail address: docdelivery@haworthpress.com].

Available online at http://jqaht.haworthpress.com
© 2006 by The Haworth Press, Inc. All rights reserved.
doi:10.1300/J162v07n01_03

KEYWORDS. Benchmarking, tourist attractions, Australia, knowledge management, performance

INTRODUCTION

Tourist attraction managers, tourists and even tourism analysts all share a potential interest in the topic of benchmarking. For each group, the assessment of the performance of a tourist attraction is made more intelligible by comparison against other operations. By themselves, comparisons and competitive considerations do not constitute benchmarking but when the performance of any one unit is set against a leading industry standard then the comparison and competitor appraisal is appropriately entitled benchmarking (Watson, 1992).

As Fuchs and Weiermair (2004) report, benchmarking has gained significant influence and currency during the 1990s and has been applied in numerous business operations. Its use in tourism is growing with applications in the hotel, catering and tour operator sectors (Hudson, 1997; Kozak & Rimmington, 1998; Ogden, 1998; Wober, 2002). Its potential application to the tourist attraction sector is of special interest in this paper.

Riechel and Haber (2004) working in Israel included tourist attractions as a part of their comparative performance studies and Mayer (2002) has assessed theme park operations with benchmarking style studies. With these exceptions, and undoubtedly allowing for some others being prepared or difficult to access, it can be suggested that the benchmarking appraisals have yet to be fully embraced in tourist attraction studies.

This paper considers the different types of benchmarking which have been identified in the literature and posits some explanations as to why the attractions sector may have made limited use of benchmarking. Additionally it develops a connection between benchmarking and knowledge management. In order to illustrate the potential value of benchmarking for the tourist attraction sector, the results of a large scale survey of Australian tourist attractions will be presented. Fifteen indicators of performance will be defined and several of these variables are illustrated in a graphic format to facilitate the kind of comparative appraisal which is at the heart of benchmarking.

TYPES OF BENCHMARKING

Scholarly opinion appears to be divided as to whether there are three or four types of benchmarking. Wober (2002) suggests there are four versions of the activity. He suggests that there is (1) internal benchmarking where functions, departments or projects in the same company or organisation are compared and (2) external benchmarking which itself is subdivided into three elements. The first kind of external benchmarking is best practice benchmarking where another organisation, regardless of its location, is singled out as the "gold" standard, a resource to be examined for its exemplary practices. A second kind of external benchmarking is competitive benchmarking where the other operations in the same business or organisational domain are considered and a relative standing obtained. There is no implication here in competitive benchmarking that the practices of any or all of the organizations studied are particularly good or particularly problematic. A third kind of external benchmarking, which completes Wober's list of four variants, is sector benchmarking. Here a quite specific sector is identified (such as all small hotels rather than the accommodation sector) and a more precise form of competitive benchmarking is achieved.

Hudson (1997) also identifies four kinds of benchmarking; the same three processes described by Wober as internal, competitive and industry (or sector) benchmarking but she does not use Wober's best practice category and instead introduces the term process benchmarking. In this approach a business having identified just one element of their operation which they deem to be of interest seeks an organisation which is known to be doing this well. Arguably Hudson's process benchmarking is a more tailored version of Wober's generic best practice benchmarking.

Fuchs and Weiermair (2004) argue for three kinds of benchmarking; process, performance and strategic. Their performance and strategic approaches appear to combine the best practice, sector and competitive notions of Hudson (1997) and Wober (2002) but the addition of a strategic dimension to the approach is somewhat novel. The researchers suggest that strategic benchmarking seeks to identify winning strategies underlying success. More generally Fuchs and Weiermair summarise the total value of benchmarking as a "catalyst" for fast learning, thus making an initial link to the present interest in knowledge management at attractions. The researcher's comment:

> Organizations who systematically seek out and study best practices may experience the beneficial effect of intellectual leverage through benchmarking. They will enjoy the effects of good ideas, creativity and innovation. (2004, p. 213)

As a further note on benchmarking, some commentators have observed that a de-facto form of benchmarking exists in the use of labels, accreditation membership and symbolic recognition systems (Font, Haas, Thorpe & Forsyth, 2001; Kozak & Nield, 2004). It is appropriate to include these accreditation systems in a discussion of benchmarking since while the key assessment criteria are usually externally imposed, rather than driven by the organisation's needs, the end result is still within the ambit of establishing comparisons against a standard.

IMPEDIMENTS TO ATTRACTION BENCHMARKING

There are several potential explanations accounting for the limited use by attractions of benchmarking ideas. As Reichel and Haber (2004) emphasise, there is considerable diversity within the attractions sector. This raises important questions concerning the definition of attractions and the kinds of related tourism businesses against which any one attraction can compare itself. Another fundamental issue is that benchmarking assumes a level of planning in tourist attraction management and there is evidence, at least in the context of Australia, that not all attraction management employs strategic planning while some hardly plan at all (Benckendorff & Pearce, 2003). A further fundamental impediment is the quality and availability of the data for benchmarking purposes. This problem is not confined to any one country but rather it varies from country to country depending on government policies, cultural norms and the availability of research providers. In China, for example, Guangrui (2003) laments the lack of openness in government policies concerning the dissemination of research data and points out that without easily accessible comparative information slow learning rather than informed knowledge management tends to prevail. In many locations there is simply no data at the government level because of difficulties in defining attractions and resourcing the research. Additionally commercial organizations can be reluctant to share information for fear of losing business (Wober, 2002). At times, more emancipated views prevail and in the Los Angeles area Pearce, Morrison and Rutledge (1998) report that major tourist attractions at least share visitor numbers seeing themselves as cooperative leisure industries rather than necessarily hostile competitors. The same collaborative approach has also been observed amongst attractions in Sydney (Benckendorff, 2004).

University researchers, as well as consultants and government officials, represent one group with the skills to conduct cross-business surveys and benchmarking for tourist attractions. The key data germane to this study was generated by inquiry driven research goals and its use as a potential benchmarking data mine for tourist attractions is a valuable applied opportunity stemming from the academic research.

Usable Knowledge

In a broad sense there has been a recognition throughout scholarly writing that knowledge is linked to power and influence. Foucault (1976) discusses local or naïve knowledge and suggests that social power struggles are rooted in conflicts for the control of ways of seeing the world. Wurman (1989), one of the authors whose work also anticipates the business-based writing on knowledge management, suggests there are five rings or circles of knowledge surrounding individuals. Like Foucault, Wurman identifies a cultural and power linked layer of influence but in addition he specifies news information, which is obtained from the media; reference information which encompasses material on systems to run the world; conversational information which are the formal and informal exchanges we have with others and, finally, internal information which is physiological and psychological responses from our own internal systems.

The present interest in benchmarking can be seen as tied to Wurman's concept of reference information but there is also an applicability in both the cultural information layer and Foucault's concern with power since cultural practices and values will determine the extent to which organizations will share data and its interpretation. During the 1990s researchers and analysts prompted by the new technologies and their communicative possibilities began to develop a coherent view of knowledge and information management. Initially there was the pivotal view that knowledge was a significant resource and the basis for future power and organisational effectiveness (Drucker, 1993; Toffler, 1990). Second, several authors delineated categories and steps in a chain of knowledge management. For example, Skyme (1996) proposes that there is a knowledge life cycle which includes (1) creation and identification, (2) organisation and assimilation, (3) application and use, (4) dissemination, and (5) protection. Other authors place more importance on the creative and innovative phases stressing the skills of the knowledge workers and their ability to apply the resources they access (Newman, 1996).

A third realisation in this sequence of work has been to recognise that knowledge management is not an end in itself, but is centrally connected to its use in a cycle of incorporation and conversion. You, O'Leary and Fesenmaier (2000) comment in reviewing work on usable knowledge approaches in Japanese companies:

> What is unique about the way these companies bring about continuous innovation is the link between the outside and the inside. Knowledge that is accumulated from the outside is shared widely within the organisation, stored as a part of the company's knowledge base and utilized by those engaged in new technologies and products. A conversion process takes place–from outside to inside and back outside again in the form of new products, services systems or targeted segments. (2000, p. 194)

Knowledge management and the concept of usable knowledge represent a contemporary answer to a question which often confronts academic researchers; the question "so what?" The issue of the relevance of research findings is an enduring critique facing many curiosity driven researchers and the knowledge management framework provides a comprehensive answer. It suggests that through shared data and technologically driven improved access, organizations can seek out much of the material they want for in-house incorporation into their business or policy decisions. In this view the relevance of academic research is expanded since published findings and data might be relevant to different industry sectors or groups, at different scales of analyses and over different time frames. More subtly, some research pieces will become permanently embedded in the organisation's operating system thus generating consequences considerably beyond any one applied research study.

STUDY AIMS

The major objective of this study of Australian tourist attractions lies in examining the broad organisational and performance characteristics of the sector. More specifically the key objective in the context of this consideration of benchmarking and usable knowledge lies in providing a competitive benchmarking data resource for attraction planners, analysts and policy makers. The material provided is best captured by the term competitive benchmarking because the relative standings of categories of attraction are being determined and there is no necessary value implication that there is a best practice in these outcomes. The values placed on the outcomes obtained will depend in part on the values of the reader or knowledge user.

METHOD

Sample

Subjects

The research focussed on Australian tourist attractions in operation between April 2000 and July 2000. The sample was selected on a non-random, convenience basis. Databases of tourist attraction contact details for each state and territory were obtained from various sources. Contact details for attractions in Queensland, South Australia, New South Wales, the Australian Capital Territory and the Northern Territory were obtained from the Internet. Contact information for attractions from Tasmania and Western Australia were received from direct correspondence with respective state tourism organizations. Victorian attraction details proved more difficult to obtain and had to be extracted from a comprehensive tourist directory prepared by the Royal Automobile Club of Victoria. The complete database resulted in over 2000 attractions.

The complete database was subjected to a filtering process to eliminate attractions that were inappropriate for the study. This filtering process was necessary because individual state databases varied in detail and classification of attractions. The filtering process allowed for a more valid sample and ensured that the study was conducted in a cost-effective manner. The types of attractions that were removed from the database included:

- *Non-managed attractions and landscape features* (such as lookouts, parks, gardens, lighthouses and picnic grounds)–It was highly unlikely that responses would be received from these attractions.
- *National Parks*–National parks are managed by a central administration in each state and it was felt that their organisational structure and responses would introduce statistical irregularities.
- *Craft shops, souvenir stores, tearooms and retail outlets* (including retail galleries)–These operations were, by definition, not considered to be attractions.
- *Markets and Festivals*–The temporary and sporadic nature of markets and festivals excluded these attractions from the study.

- *Wineries*–After careful deliberation wineries were excluded from the sample as they were viewed as not being representative of most attractions. It was felt that the large number of wineries in the original database would have introduced highly irregular results.

The filtered database resulted in a total sample of 1665 attractions. The distribution by state is summarised in Table 1. Values for state population, international visitor numbers and domestic visitor numbers are also provided as a basis for comparison. The figures indicate that population size and visitor numbers are closely related to the number of attractions each state can support. To further explore this argument a simple Pearson correlation was performed. The correlation indicated that the number of attractions per state was highly correlated with population, international visitor numbers and domestic visitor numbers, with all correlation coefficients being higher than 0.90. This provides support for the argument that the study sample has been accurately represented.

Profile of Responses

A total of 1665 questionnaires were sent by standard mail in April, 2000. At the conclusion of the study in July 2000, 430 responses had been received. Of these, 23 were deemed to be invalid. Questionnaires were deemed to be invalid if they were returned by establishments that were excluded from the study. A further 55 (3.3%) questionnaires were returned undelivered, indicating that 1610 questionnaires reached their

TABLE 1. State by State Comparison of Attraction Numbers, Population and Visitor Numbers

	Attractions (2000)	Population (1999)	International Visitors (1999)	Overnight Domestic Visitors (1999)
New South Wales and ACT	441	6 762 900	1 574 378	28 525 000
Victoria	350	4 741 500	787 189	16 670 000
Queensland	254	3 539 500	952 913	16 362 000
Western Australia	246	1 873 800	455 741	5 426 000
South Australia	168	1 495 800	165 724	6 443 000
Tasmania	155	469 900	82 862	2 047 000
Northern Territory	51	194 300	124 293	991 000
TOTAL	1665	19 077 700	4 143 100	76 464 000

destination. This was a good indication that the database was largely accurate. A summary of responses is provided in Table 2.

The response rate for the questionnaires that were delivered was 26.7%. This was within the expected response range of 20% to 30%.

Attraction Type

A large number of attractions (49.6%) responding to the questionnaire were museums. Table 3 provides a more detailed breakdown of responses. The categories presented are not mutually exclusive. Attraction managers were able to select any number of categories that best described their attraction. Consequently many museums may have selected both *Museum* and *Australian Culture and History*. This approach recognises that many attractions are diversifying to provide tourists with a compelling mix of entertainment and education and thus cannot be restricted to a single category.

While the number of museums appears to be disproportionate to other types of attractions anecdotal evidence supports the findings. It is not uncommon to find small museums administered by historical societies in many Australian towns. Many typical small Australian towns often boast a museum as their only attraction. A Tourism New South Wales (1999) study of 100 attractions found that museums and historical sites (18%) were the second most common category after nature-based attractions (27%). Many larger regional centres also support art galleries (12.8%) managed by a local society or shire council. This compares with 16% for the Tourism New South Wales study.

TABLE 2. Response Rates to Tourist Attraction Questionnaire

	Dispatched	Delivered	Responses	
	n	n	n	%
New South Wales and ACT	441	426	90	21.1
Victoria	350	333	92	27.6
Queensland	254	249	67	26.9
Western Australia	246	236	49	20.8
South Australia	168	167	46	27.5
Tasmania	155	153	35	22.8
Northern Territory	51	46	11	23.9
State not indicated			17	1.1
Invalid			23	1.4
TOTAL	**1665**	**1610**	**430**	**26.7**

TABLE 3. Comparison of Responses by Attraction Type

Attraction Category	N	%
Listed Categories		
Museums	186	49.6
Australian culture/history	140	37.3
Galleries	48	12.8
Farming	47	12.5
Nature-based attractions	45	12.0
Wildlife parks / aquaria	40	10.7
Gardens	37	9.9
Theme parks	31	8.3
National trust	28	7.5
Action/adventure	24	6.4
Factory/manufacturing	20	5.3
Military	17	4.5
Casinos	1	0.3
Other		
Specialist attractions	43	11.2
Interpretive/information	12	3.1
Railway-based	9	2.3
Mining/fossicking	6	1.6
Science/astronomy	4	1.0

The questionnaire also received a high response from *farming* attractions (12.5%). This figure excludes wineries, as indicated previously. The inclusion of wineries would no doubt result in a large number of attractions that could be placed under a broader "agriculture" banner. Typical farming attractions include larger establishments, such as Queensland's "Big Pineapple," as well as smaller operations, such as local strawberry farms, animal farms and other agricultural attractions. The Tourism New South Wales study found that 8% of attractions were based on agriculture (excluding wineries).

Nature-based attractions also account for 12% of responses to the questionnaire. Continued visitor interest in ecotourism and nature-based attractions has created strong demand for this type of attraction.

Wildlife attractions (10.7%) and gardens (9.9%) also accounted for a surprisingly high number of responses while military attractions (4.5%) accounted for fewer establishments. Only one casino responded to the questionnaire.

Attractions in the 'other' category (19.6%) included information, educational and interpretive centres (3.1%), railway-based attractions

(3.3%), mining and fossicking (1.6%), science and astronomy (1.0%) and various specialist attractions (11.2%).

Treatment of Statistical Outliers

The diverse nature of the attraction sector inherently results in individual establishments that stand out or are inconsistent with general trends and patterns. These 'outliers' can skew and bias findings and frustrate attempts to draw inferences about the original population. Barnet and Lewis (1994, p. 7) define outliers as:

> An observation (or subset of observations) which appears to be inconsistent with the remainder of that set of data.

The issue of outliers is important because researchers are faced with making an objective judgement about whether a particular case is an outlier or a *bona fide* member of the sample. The scope of this study, however, is to provide an undistorted overview of Australian visitor attractions. The presence of a few extreme outliers creates statistical inconsistencies which can grossly distort measures of central tendency and associated statistical analyses.

Barnett and Lewis (1994) identify three approaches to processing outliers: they can be rejected, adjusted or simply left unaltered.

Given the aims of this study the approach that has been adopted is to reject outliers. While there are many methodologies for rejecting outliers (Barnett & Lewis, 1994), the method employed in this study involved the elimination of cases that deviated from the mean by more than two standard deviations. According to the *empirical rule*, about 95% of values in any distribution will lie within two standard deviations of the mean (Freund & Simon, 1992). Thus, the methodology employed in the study resulted in the elimination of cases in the lower 2.5 percent and upper 2.5 percent of a distribution. This procedure was only applied to measures where outliers were clearly apparent.

Survey Content

The questionnaire completed by the attraction managers sought information on the following key variables. These factors were considered to be the basic elements necessary for effective benchmarking appraisals across the attraction sector in Australia. The key factors that were assessed are shown in Table 4.

TABLE 4. Basic Benchmarking Factors for Tourist Attractions

Factors	Description
Visitor factors	
Visitor numbers	The number of visitors to the attraction in the year prior to the study
Visitor growth	The growth in visitor numbers, measure on a 3-point scale ranging from increasing to decreasing.
Visitor length of stay	An estimate of the length of time spent by visitors at the attraction (in minutes)
Visitor market origin	The distribution of visitors from local, state, national and international origins
Group visitation	The percentage of visitors who are part of an organised group
Financial Factors	
Gross revenue	The gross annual income for the attraction
Total profit	The attraction's net annual profit after meeting expenses and tax obligations
Asset value	The estimated net worth of the attraction
Revenue sources	The percentage split between 12 different revenue sources
Admission prices	The adult, child, family and concession prices for entering the attraction
Employment factors	
Volunteers	The number of volunteers working at the attraction
Paid employees	The total number of casual, part-time and full-time staff employed by the attraction
Age of the attraction	The age of the attraction in years

In addition to the questions asking for this factual or objective information respondents were also asked to rate their attractions in relation to their perceived competitors. This subjective measure of performance was assessed by using a rating scale of 1 (very good) to 5 (very poor) to determine respondents' perceptions of:

1. quality of attraction
2. relationship with local community
3. employee satisfaction
4. total asset base
5. diversification
6. development of new elements
7. market share
8. total revenue
9. growth in visitor numbers
10. net profit

RESULTS

The presentation of information in this section is organised by using the different attraction themes as an organising principle. Additionally, since the aim of this study is to provide a competitive benchmarking data resource, key comparative information is provided for all the principle variables collected. In order to avoid excessive duplication and to enhance the benchmarking applicability of the study, key data on (1) visitor factors, (2) financial factors, (3) employment factors, (4) subjective performance, and (5) complexity of attraction operation environment are provided.

Visitor Factors

Information on visitor numbers and visitor growth organised by attraction theme is presented in Figure 1.

The visitor growth/attendance matrix indicates how groups within the attraction sector are performing. The matrix uses mean growth and attendance values to present a visual model of the attraction sector. It should be noted that due to only one response, the casino category has been excluded from the matrix to maintain the integrity of the data. All other categories received more than ten responses.

Information on visitor numbers and length of stay at the attraction is provided in Figure 2.

Information on visitor origins can also be related to the type of attraction and this data is provided in Figure 3.

A final view of visitor comparisons is provided in Figure 4, where the percentage of group visitors is recorded against visitor numbers for the attraction types.

Financial Factors

An understanding of the financial performance of Australian tourist attractions was undertaken initially by contrasting for the attraction categories the relative mean total profits compared to the managers' stated response to the attractions asset value. This material is provided in Figure 5.

Additional financial performance factors can be understood through cross referencing mean total profit and mean asset value. This material is provided in Figure 6.

In order to complete the relationships among the financial factors it is also possible to present the relationship between mean gross revenue

FIGURE 1. Visitor Numbers/Visitor Growth Matrix for Attraction Categories

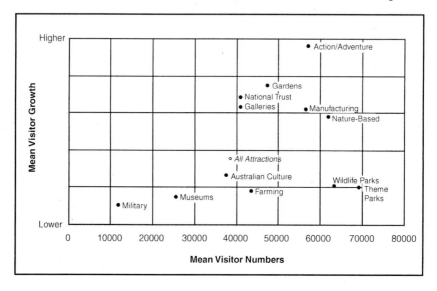

FIGURE 2. Visitor Numbers/Length of Stay Matrix for Attraction Categories

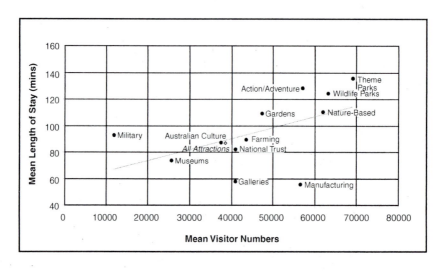

FIGURE 3. Origin of Visitors Based on Attraction Type

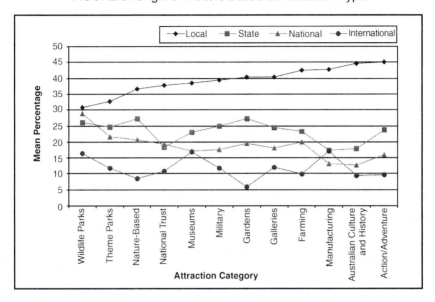

FIGURE 4. Visitor Numbers/Group Visitation Matrix for Attraction Categories

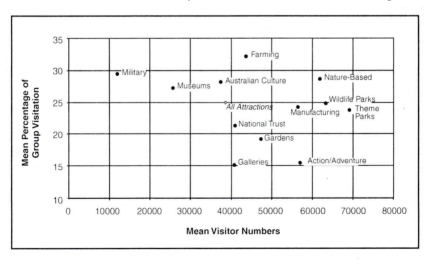

FIGURE 5. Mean Total Profit/Mean Asset Value Matrix for Attraction Categories

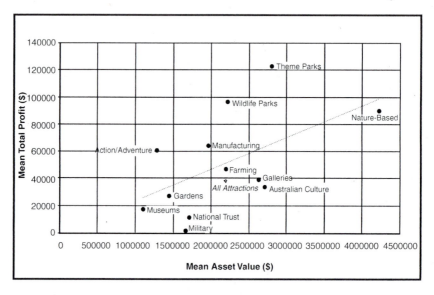

FIGURE 6. Mean Total Profit/Mean Gross Revenue Matrix for Attraction Categories

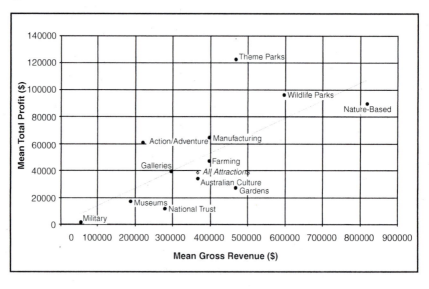

and mean asset value. This material is presented in Figure 7 and largely confirms the pattern of attraction performance in Figures 5 and 6.

A further understanding of the financial performance of the attractions is provided by considering the admission prices of attractions. This material is provided in Figure 8.

A contextual variable likely to be of some influence in relation to financial performance is that of the age of the attraction. The relevant data is provided in Figure 9.

Employment Factors

The two key factors assessed in describing employment, the mean number of paid employees and the mean number of volunteers are cross-referenced in Figure 10.

Subjective Measures of Performance

In order to integrate the attraction managers' ratings of their financial performance the ten perceived performance measures were factor ana-

FIGURE 7. Mean Gross Revenue/Mean Asset Value Matrix for Attraction Categories

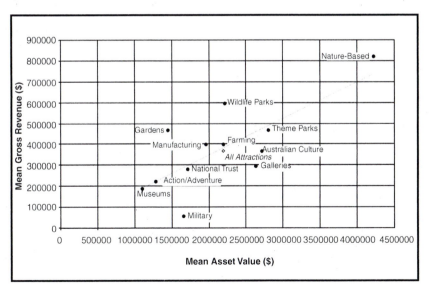

FIGURE 8. Mean Admission Prices for Adults, Children and Concessions Split by Attraction Type

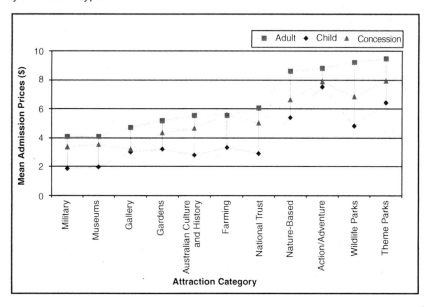

FIGURE 9. Attraction Age/Management Tenure Matrix for Attraction Categories

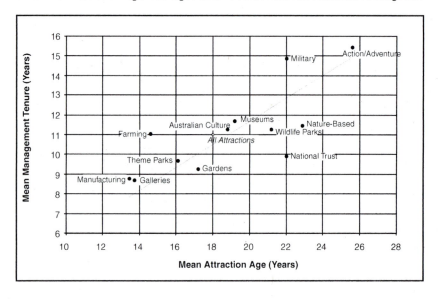

FIGURE 10. Volunteers/Paid Employees Matrix for Attraction Categories

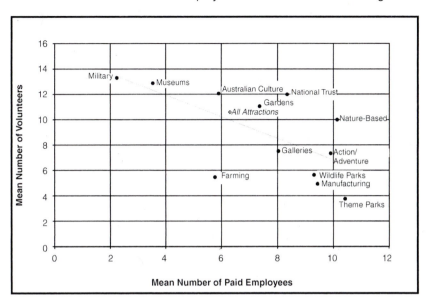

lysed. The results of the factor analysis are presented in Table 5. The three significant factors were named size, growth and social responsibility and accounted for 25 percent, 21 percent and 16 percent of the variance respectively.

These factors were then related to the attraction types and the relative performance of the attractions were recorded. This material is provided in Figure 11.

A final overview of the main elements of the data presented in this appraisal can be summarised by a table which converts the numerical data into categorical or nominal appraisals. By considering whether each attraction type is above or below the mean value on all the characteristics considered so far a comprehensive overview of the attractions can be obtained. The relevant summary information is presented in Table 6.

DISCUSSION

This study has attempted to provide a comprehensive competitive benchmarking data resource pertaining to Australian tourist attractions.

TABLE 5. Rotated Factor Correlation Matrix for Perceived Performance Scales

Perceived Performance Measures	Mean[a]	Performance Factors		
		Size	Growth	Social Responsibility
Total revenue	2.78	**0.850**	0.121	0.095
Net profit	2.92	**0.848**	0.028	0.046
Market Share (Number of Visitors)	2.71	**0.671**	0.215	0.193
Total asset base	2.27	**0.550**	0.245	−0.028
Diversification	2.33	0.164	**0.860**	0.040
Development of New Elements	2.36	0.058	**0.799**	0.261
Growth in visitor numbers	2.65	0.387	**0.568**	0.095
Relationship with the local community	1.72	−0.003	−0.001	**0.863**
Employee Satisfaction	1.93	0.127	0.278	**0.739**
Quality of Attraction	1.65	0.337	0.410	**0.428**
Aggregate Factor Mean[a]		2.67	2.45	1.78

[a]Mean is based on the following scale: *1 = Very Good, 5 = Very poor*

FIGURE 11. Aggregate Size, Growth and Social Responsibility Performance Ratings by Attraction Type

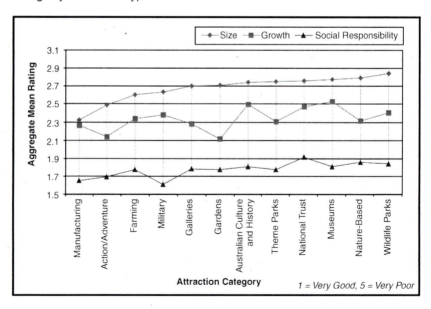

TABLE 6. Summary of Attraction Characteristics by Attraction Type

	Visitor Numbers	Visitor Growth	Length of Stay	Gross Revenue	Profit	Asset Value	Paid Employees	Volunteers	Size	Growth	Social Responsibility
Museums	−	−	−	−	−	−	−	+	+	−	+
Australian Culture	−	−	+	−	−	+	−	+	+	−	+
Military	−	−	+	−	−	−	−	+	−	−	−
National Trust	+	+	−	−	−	−	+	+	+	−	+
Action/Adventure	+	+	+	−	+	−	+	−	−	+	−
Manufacturing	+	+	−	+	+	−	+	−	−	+	−
Farming	+	−	+	+	+	+	−	−	−	−	+
Galleries	+	+	−	−	+	+	+	−	−	+	−
Gardens	+	+	+	+	−	−	+	+	−	+	−
Theme Parks	+	−	+	+	+	+	+	−	+	+	−
Wildlife Parks and Aquaria	+	−	+	+	+	+	+	−	+	+	+
Nature−Based	+	+	+	+	+	+	+	−	+	+	+

[+] above overall mean; [−] below overall mean

It was not a hypothesis driven study but rather an exploratory effort laying out patterns of characteristics concerning attractions as reported by a large sample of attraction managers. The use and applicability of such material can be illustrated from an analyst's perspective by focussing on one attraction type–wildlife parks and aquaria–and locating the performance of these types of attractions within the larger tourism framework.

The data reported in all the tables and figures pertaining to the attraction themes and summarised in a qualitative manner in Table 6 provides the following benchmarking information on wildlife parks and aquaria. It suggests that they are distinctive in their performance and their managers' perception of performance. They exceed the mean of Australian tourist attraction performance in terms of visitor numbers, gross revenue, profit, asset value and the number of paid employees. Visitors to wildlife parks and aquaria stay longer than average and the attractions are larger in size, better in growth potential and exhibit more social responsibility. They also have fewer volunteers than the average tourist attraction. All of these average or comparative assignments can be quantified more precisely from the data in the relevant figures and tables.

The preceding level of analysis reported for wildlife parks and aquaria is somewhat typical of the academic or researcher appraisal of tourist settings. Researchers seek to provide models, generalisations and inductive or deductive accounts of tourism phenomenon in their roles as knowledge innovators and organisers. A distinction can be drawn between this kind of knowledge involvement and that of a practitioner or operator. For example, an individual investing in or managing a wildlife park or aquaria might find the comparative figures with other attractions broadly appealing but is very likely to want more precise information on the variability of wildlife parks themselves. That is the information request and knowledge gap identified is focussed and particularistic. In terms of the kinds of information developed in this paper an even more fine-grained view is required and like a map or photograph, the need for a different level of detail or resolution is required.

There are some implications arising from this study concerning the problems and lessons involved in developing benchmarks. As Wober (2002) has highlighted, the selection of comparable properties or organizations represents several challenges. Not only is there an issue in terms of which properties are desirable to assess either in terms of best practice or competitive standards, but also ethical issues involving the cooperation of these properties are pivotal. Importantly, few studies have addressed what kinds of incentives might function well to stimulate cooperation. Should benchmarking be achieved through payment, should mutual or conditional access to the findings be engineered as a part of the cooperative approach or is it acceptable to collect benchmarking data surreptitiously through such activities as mystery shoppers, former employee interviews or cross-firm recruitment? Importantly what role should government and academic researchers play in providing quality, freely accessible public information which private businesses can then use for purely corporate gains? Benchmarking, as one technique for knowledge sharing and quality control, quickly introduces these issues of ethics and power. Until such issues are debated widely and government-researcher-industry standards on acceptable codes of behaviour more fully developed it is likely that the rich potential of benchmarking to assist quality performance may be hindered. A rich debate on the ethics, practices and needs which underlie benchmarking would appear to be a necessary next step for the business and tourism research-user community.

REFERENCES

Barnett, V. and Lewis, T. (1994) Outliers in statistical data (Third Edition). Chichester: Wiley.

Benckendorff, P.J. (2004) *Planning for the Future: A Profile of Australian Tourist Attractions.* Unpublished PhD Dissertation. Townsville: James Cook University.

Benckendorff, P.J., & Pearce, P.L. (2003). Australian tourism attractions: The links between organisational characteristics and planning. *Journal of Travel Research*, *42*(1), 24-35.

Drucker, P.F. (1993). *Post-Capitalist Society.* New York: Harper Business.

Font, X., Haas, E., Thorpe, K., & Forsyth, L (2001). Directory of tourism ecolabels. In X. Font & R. Buckley (Eds), *Tourism Ecolabelling: Certification and Promotion of Sustainable Management.* Wallingford: CABI.

Foucault, M. (1976). *Power/Knowledge.* New York: Pantheon Books.

Freund, J.E. and Simon, G.A. (1992) Modern Elementary Statistics (Eight Edition). New Jersey: Prentice-Hall.

Fuchs, M. & Weiermair, K. (2004). Destination benchmarking: An indicator-system's potential for exploring guest satisfaction. *Journal of Travel Research*, 42, 212-225.

Guangrui, Z. (2003). Tourism research in China. In A. Lew, L. Yu, J. Ap & Z. Guangrui (Eds), *Tourism in China* (pp. 67-82). New York: The Haworth Hospitality Press.

Hudson, P. (1997). *Benchmarking and Best Practice Among Tour Operators in Northern Australia.* Townsville: Northern Australia Social research Institute.

Kozak, M., & Nield, K. (2004). The role of quality and eco-labelling systems in destination benchmarking. *Journal of Sustainable Tourism*, 12(2), 138-148.

Kozak, M., & Rimmington, M. (1998). Benchmarking: Destination attractiveness and small hospitality business performance. *International Journal of Contemporary Hospitality Management*, 10(5), 74-8.

Mayer, K.J. (2002). Human resource practices and service quality in theme parks. *International Journal of Contemporary Hospitality Management*, 14(4), 169-175.

Newman, B. (1996). Cited in You, X., O'Leary, J., & Fesenmaier, D. (2000). Knowledge management through the web: A new marketing paradigm for tourism organizations. In B. Faulkner, G. Moscardo & E. Laws (Eds), *Tourism in the 21st Century* (pp. 181-197). London: Continuum.

Ogden, S. (1998). Comment: Benchmarking and best practice in the small hotel sector. *International Journal of Contemporary Hospitality Management*, 10(5), 189-190.

Pearce, P.L., Morrison, A., & Rutledge, J. (1998). *Tourism: Bridges Across Continents.* Sydney, Australia: McGraw-Hill.

Reichel, A., & Haber, S. (2004). A three-sector comparison of the business performance of small tourism enterprises: An exploratory study. *Tourism Management.* [On-line] Available: doi:10.1016/j.tourman.2004.03.017.

Skyme, D.J. (1996). Cited in You, X., O'Leary, J., & Fesenmaier, D. (2000). Knowledge management through the web: A new marketing paradigm for tourism organizations. In B. Faulkner, G. Moscardo & E. Laws (Eds), *Tourism in the 21st Century* (pp. 181-197). London: Continuum.

Toffler, A. (1990). *Powershift: Knowledge, Wealth and Violence at the Edge of the 21st Century*. New York: Bantam Books.

Tourism New South Wales (1999) Attractions Development Strategy for Regional New South Wales: Towards a successful New South Wales Attractions Sector. Sydney: Tourism New South Wales.

Watson, G.H. (1992). *The Benchmarking Workbook: adopting Best Practices for Performance Improvement*. Portland, Oregon: Productivity Press.

Wober, K. (2002). *Benchmarking in Tourism and Hospitality Industries*. Wallingford, Oxon: CABI.

Wurman, R.S. (1989). *Information Anxiety*. New York: Doubleday.

You, X., O'Leary, J., & Fesenmaier, D. (2000). Knowledge management through the web: A new marketing paradigm for tourism organizations. In B. Faulkner, G. Moscardo & E. Laws (Eds), *Tourism in the 21st Century* (pp. 181-197). London: Continuum.

doi:10.1300/J162v07n01_03

Response Quality of E-Mail Inquiries– A Driver for Knowledge Management in the Tourism Organization?

Anita Zehrer
Harald Pechlaner

SUMMARY. The growing world-wide competition of tourism regions, changing demand patterns, the claim for better products and offers, the decreasing attractiveness and increasing uniformity of offers consistently lead to new challenges for the quality assurance of destinations. High service quality enables tourism entrepreneurs to achieve decisive competitive advantages. Quality within a destination comprises all services which the guest is engaged in and is not limited by time or location of the stay. A crucial point is the first contact of a guest with the destination, which happens by e-mail inquiries in the majority of cases. The development of information technology has lead to more and more guests gathering pieces of information via the internet and has induced researchers to study this phenomenon (Buhalis and Licata, 2002; Raman-Bacchus and Molina, 2001). Therefore, response behavior becomes a key

Anita Zehrer teaches Tourism Business Studies, Management Center Innsbruck, University of Applied Sciences, Weiherburggasse 8, 6020 Innsbruck, Austria (E-mail: anita.zehrer@mci.edu). Harald Pechlaner is Foundation Professor of Tourism, Catholic University of Eichstaett-Ingolstadt, Pater-Philipp-Jeningen-Platz 2, 85071, Eichstaett, Germany (E-mail: harald.pechlaner@ku-eichstaett.de).

[Haworth co-indexing entry note]: "Response Quality of E-Mail Inquiries–A Driver for Knowledge Management in the Tourism Organization?" Zehrer, Anita, and Harald Pechlaner. Co-published simultaneously in *Journal of Quality Assurance in Hospitality & Tourism* (The Haworth Hospitality Press, an imprint of The Haworth Press, Inc.) Vol. 7, No. 1/2, 2006, pp. 53-73; and: *Knowledge Sharing and Quality Assurance in Hospitality and Tourism* (ed: Noel Scott and Eric Laws) The Haworth Hospitality Press, an imprint of The Haworth Press, Inc., 2006, pp. 53-73. Single or multiple copies of this article are available for a fee from The Haworth Document Delivery Service [1-800-HAWORTH, 9:00 a.m. - 5:00 p.m. (EST). E-mail address: docdelivery@haworthpress.com].

Available online at http://jqaht.haworthpress.com
© 2006 by The Haworth Press, Inc. All rights reserved.
doi:10.1300/J162v07n01_04

factor for the success of tourism organizations (Pechlaner et al. 2002). From the guest's point of view, the speed of response and breadth of information are to be seen as decisive factors for service quality and customer satisfaction. A mystery guest check by means of e-mail inquiries sent to selected tourism organizations was undertaken to determine the response behaviour and breadth of information provided by tourism organizations and to reveal potential gaps in the knowledge management and transfer of these organizations. According to elaborated quality criteria and standards, the paper reports a two-year mystery guest study of tourism organizations of an Alpine destination in Europe. doi:10.1300/J162v07n01_04 *[Article copies available for a fee from The Haworth Document Delivery Service: 1-800-HAWORTH. E-mail address: <docdelivery@haworthpress.com> Website: <http://www.HaworthPress.com> © 2006 by The Haworth Press, Inc. All rights reserved.]*

KEYWORDS. E-mail-based communication, quality in tourism, tourism organizations, knowledge management in tourism

INTRODUCTION

In recent years, tourism has been confronted with two main developments–changes in consumer behaviour and changes in modern information and communication technologies. This situation has led to a big challenge for tourism actors, particularly for tourism organizations, for which the effective management of information technology is fundamental.

First, consumer behavior has changed considerably during recent years. Better services are required, up-to-date product information is requested, more specific offers are demanded, guests are becoming more mobile, critical and more price-sensitive, they compare offers, tend to spend more but shorter vacations, and decide later on where to spend their holidays. These changes in consumer behaviour structure lead to a decreased time span between booking and consumption and entail new challenges in tourism, like information creation and distribution, product creation, performance evaluation, planning and forecasting, and flexible as well as mobile user access to support the planning and decision making procedure of the "new" tourist (Pechlaner and Tschurtschenthaler, 2003). The new tourist is more and more independent and expects tailored holidays with all comforts, maximum quality, a good trade-off with regard to price and performance, accurate information and a unique experience.

Second, the identification of e-mail-based (commercial) communications in tourism is quite pertinent and the context of competition and changing consumption patterns is highly relevant. Information Technology (IT) innovations literally force us to reconsider the task of communication and the tourism industry must meet the challenges of competitiveness. Quality has become a key element in tourism (Smeral, 1998). Integrated quality management has to be recognized as an essential component in a strategy for actions which aims at the competitiveness of tourism organizations. Quality management contributes to growth, to employment and to the sustainable and balanced development of the destination. Hence, quality in tourism has many dimensions. Through quality management, efforts are being made to take account of the growing importance of individual aspects of quality. Moreover, quality of the tourism product cannot be achieved without the appropriate skills and a certain extent of motivation of tourism employees. The importance of life-long learning and of the social dialogue becomes evident. Generally, it can be stated that on the global online market place particularly e-mail has become the leading internet application and activity in tourism (Wei et al., 2001). Furthermore, electronic communication channels have obtained a crucial position in customer relationship management (CRM).

QUALITY MANAGEMENT OF TOURISM SERVICES

Today there are an increasing number of countries and regions that are investigating and investing in this area. Quality is a cross-cutting issue of great significance for competition, trade, sustainability and ethics. Following the example of tourism companies, the issue of quality has been addressed only recently in the agenda of tourism destinations which are aware that the condition of their tourism product is the sum of contributions and processes resulting from many stakeholders, both private and public. Decision-makers in tourism policies and strategies are nevertheless facing a difficult task because there is no overall and unquestionable international standard but rather a variety of options, which may lead to similar quality objectives. Significant case studies are therefore available, but their adaptation to someone else's specific needs cannot be immediate as each destination and each tourism company aims at different contents, types and levels of quality corresponding to different market segments.

Quality is a homonym, a term with a wide range of definitions. It is a complex and multifaceted notion (Garvin, 1984). The term has become one of the main catchwords and many developments have taken place around this concept in recent years. Quality definitions arise from different traditions. The management of quality has emerged as an important theme in business management during the past 50 years and is gaining in importance in all areas of modern life. In tourism too, guests require top-quality products and value-for-money services. The further reasons for systematic quality management in tourism are widely documented: growing competition, lack of willingness to provide a service, growing loss of individuality by the standardization of products, adverse price-performance ratio etc. However, quality in tourism is an extremely complex phenomenon. From a guest's point of view, tourism services are always the totality of a whole package of individual services (Figure 1).

Like a chain, these services are all linked: first information request from a tourist office prior to the journey, the travel to the destination, stay in vacation hotel, eating in a restaurant, mountain-railway excursions and, lastly, the trip home. Each individual service leaves its mark on and influences the overall holiday experience. Also, at the level of the individual hotel, a guest experiences the whole service package as a chain in which one service is linked to the next: information, arrival, check-in, moving into the room, dining in the restaurant, check-out. These service chains, which are specific to guests, provide an aid for systematic checking of a hotel's services and processes, showing where practical quality improvements can be made and promoting the introduction of appropriate measures. Providing services and direct contact with guests are exacting tasks because each guest has his specific expectations, needs and opinions. If these needs are not fulfilled, the guest is not satisfied with the service. Such occurrences are described as 'critical incidents;' these are defects of varying degrees in a service chain which result in failure to satisfy guests' expectations and hence trigger dissatisfaction. Customer satisfaction plays an important role in each service provider and is a major focus for tourism organizations. Anderson and Sullivan even consider investment into customer satisfaction as a kind of insurance and state that "investing in customer satisfaction is like taking out an insurance policy. If some hardship temporarily befalls the [tourism organization], customers [and/or tourists] will be more likely to remain loyal" (Anderson and Sullivan, 1993, p. 140).

FIGURE 1. Tasks of a Tourism Organization

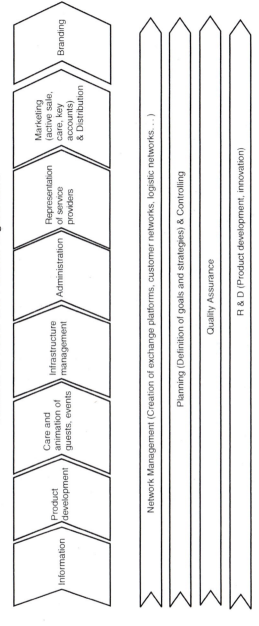

Information | Product development | Care and animation of guests, events | Infrastructure management | Administration | Representation of service providers | Marketing (active sale, care, key accounts) & Distribution | Branding

Network Management (Creation of exchange platforms, customer networks, logistic networks. . .)

Planning (Definition of goals and strategies) & Controlling

Quality Assurance

R & D (Product development, innovation)

Source: Pechlaner and Abfalter 2001: 137.

57

The Kano model of customer satisfaction classifies service attributes based on how they are perceived by customers and how they influence customer satisfaction (Kano et al., 1984). The Kano model divides service attributes into three categories: basic factors (treshhold), performance factors and excitement factors (Figure 2). A competitive product meets basic attributes, maximises performances attributes, and disposes of as many excitement attributes as possible at a cost the market can bear.

Threshold attributes (also called basic factors, dissatisfiers, minimum requirements) are the expected attributes or "musts" of a product, and do not provide an opportunity for product differentiation. Increasing the performance of these attributes provides diminishing returns in terms of customer satisfaction; however the absence or poor performance of these attributes results in extreme customer dissatisfaction. Performance attributes (i.e. bivalent dissatisfiers, hybrids) are those for which more is generally better, and will improve customer satisfaction. Conversely, a lacking or weak performance attribute reduces customer satisfaction. Of the needs customers verbalise, the majority can be seen as performance attributes. These attributes form the weighted needs against which service concepts are evaluated. Excitement attributes (i.e. satisfiers, enhancing factors) are unspoken and unexpected by custom-

FIGURE 2. The Kano Model of Customer Satisfaction

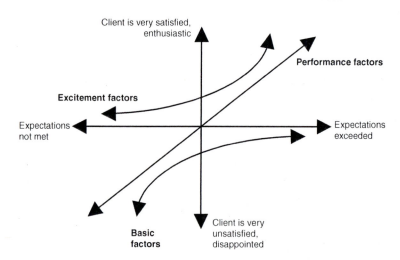

Source: Kano et al. 1984: 43.

ers but can result in high levels of customer satisfaction, however their absence does not lead to dissatisfaction. Excitement attributes often satisfy latent needs–real needs of which customers are currently unaware. The big challenge for tourism quality management in Alpine tourism destinations is to create excitement factors and to bind the guest to the destination already during his first stay. This may only be achieved if tourism organizations dispose of an eficient knowledge management.

KNOWLEDGE MANAGEMENT
IN TOURISM ORGANIZATIONS

Sigala et al. (2001) conclude that employees are confronted with new tasks demanding new skills and competences. These tasks can mainly be summarized under the catchword of knowledge management. Knowledge management is largely discussed in the literature and basically defined as a process of capturing and sharing knowledge among people to create additional value (Pechlaner et al., 2002; Dunning, 1993). Gurteen defines knowledge management as a "business philosophy–an engaging in his definition set of principles, processes, organizational structures, and technology applications that help people share and leverage their knowledge to meet their business objectives" (Gurteen, 1999, p. 3). The four main components of a knowledge management system are a knowledge sharing culture, incentives to retain employees, alliances for knowledge acquisition and a written knowledge management policy. To overcome competitive disadvantages due to diseconomies of scale, tourism organizations have to recognize the importance of effective knowledge management and knowledge sharing within destination networks.

According to Bolinger and Smith (2001) organizational knowledge can be defined as a strategic asset. If organizations wish to remain competitive, they should develop processes for capturing relevant knowledge, dispersing it correctly, periodically, concisely and at appropriate times. Knowledge within an organization is information pooled with the experience of members and depends on the situation and people involved (Von Krogh et al., 2000). Knowledge management discusses the need to identify, generate, use, exchange and collect the knowledge necessary to respond in a flexible way to market changes and new challenges. New information and communication technologies (ICT) including internet technologies ease the process of generating and transferring knowledge within networks. Technology, therefore, plays a crucial transformational role and is a key part of knowledge management (Gurteen, 1999). This comes true also for tourism organizations which have started to apply modern information technology more and more. Increasing distribution via the internet has resulted in n increasing number of guests making their inquiries and reservations online. Reaction and/or response to online inquiries become decisive, for both reasons: on the one hand, because of its influences on the customer's satisfaction–if booking is considered an element of quality–and on the other hand, because of its direct effects on the booking behavior.

Knowledge management goes into the question of what kinds of knowledge activities are inherent in an organization (Krogh et al., 2000). Knowledge activities comprise knowledge generation, knowledge use and knowledge transfer. The process of knowledge generation is especially crucial, as the number of persons included in this process and mutually interacting leads to an increase in knowledge (Nonaka and Takeuchi, 1995). The more people are involved in the knowledge generation process the bigger the knowledge spiral grows (Malkotra, 2000). Additionally, it is postulated that knowledge increase in destinations depends on size (Bieger, 1998). Small tourism organizations therefore are likely to have problems in processing the information they receive (Pechlaner and Tschurtschenthaler, 2003). The objective of this study is to present the reaction of tourism organizations to internet inquiries in order to understand the knowledge transfer mechanisms in tourism organizations. As a methodological approach, the authors make use of a "mystery guest," which is a widely used technique for the quality assessment of services and for the evaluation of service standards (Pechlaner et al., 2002).

METHODOLOGY

Mystery guest studies and mystery shopper or silent shopper programs, a form of participant observation, are regarded as a tool for evaluating and improving customer service quality (Figure 3). While service standards are set by head-office staff and management, the task of delivering the work falls to individual customer-facing employees. "Mystery shopping programs are not an arbitrary attempt to spy on employees but rather a well-elaborated plan which serves as a management tool for improving customer service as well as enhancing human resource management" (Erstad, 1998, p. 38). Wilson argued that "an encounter involves interaction, and the quality of that interaction is as dependent on the customer as it is on the service provider" (Wilson, 1998, p. 416). There are numerous objectives for choosing this kind of program: first, to shed light on front-line customer contacts; second, to enable marketers scrutinize the human element; third, to track the progress of training; fourth, to unveil how employee contact with customers is positive; and fifth, to identify areas that need training or further training.

Mystery shopping is based on a technique often used by retail stores. Retailers often hire someone to visit their own stores or a competitor's store and report on the encounter. In case of a mystery shopping program in a store or a restaurant, a mystery shopper is assigned to make a particular purchase, for example, and then communicate the experience. Mystery shopping or mystery guests programs can be regarded as a technique that aims to collect facts rather than perceptions. Mystery shopping is a special managerial tool to identify any possible defects or flaws within the customer related operations and procedures (Wilson 1998). It is generally agreed that mystery research delivers unequivocal results with regard to the achievement of objectives for internal processes. Mystery shopping is performed to determine whether a business is meeting the needs of both its customers and clients, and the business itself. Apart from mystery shoppers which are acting physically, there are methods like the mystery guest approach via e-mail inquiries, where a potential customer makes an inquiry via e-mail.

"Information requests via e-mail allow for customized questions at any time of the day. . ." (Matzler et al., 2005, p. 250). The response behaviour of tourism organizations on e-mail inquiries is a central quality element, as in the majority of cases it is the first contact to the guest (Zeithaml, Parasuraman and Malhotra, 2002). If an e-mail inquiry is not answered in a satisfactory way, the attitude of the customer with regard to the destination will change. The first impression is automatically included into the quality perception of the destination. According to Garvin, there are five quality notions (Garvin, 1984): transcendent quality, product-based quality, customer-based quality, manufacturing-based quality and value-based quality. The following figure shows an overview of the quality notions and respective measurement methods.

The use of mystery guests is related to the manufacturing quality notion, which originates from quality security and control of the production industry. All manufacturing-based quality definitions identify quality as "conformance to requirements." Accordingly, the performed service has to fulfill the rules and requirements in order to guarantee high quality. The mystery guest approach is basically used to reveal the

FIGURE 3. Service Quality Measurement Methods

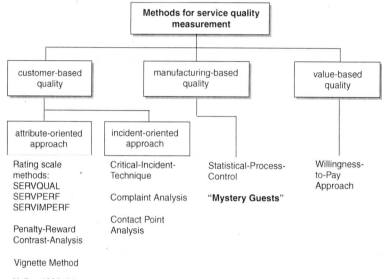

Source: Haller, 1995: 91.

behaviour of employees in a customer contact point situation. The assessment of the service quality is made in a natural environment without the tested person or organization being informed about the test situation. For guaranteeing the anonymity of the e-mail inquiries, the following prerequisites have to be met: (a) the customer contact situation has to be as realistic as possible, (b) the text has to be chosen according to the characteristics of potential guests, and (c) the service delivery process has to be divided into its single phases.

In summary, the use of the mystery guest approach is suitable for assessing the subjective quality perception of the guest. Last but not least, the use of mystery guests assumes that the quality perception of clients may be assessed in a reliable and valid way. e-mail has several advantages compared to traditional direct marketing, as it costs significantly less and is faster to send than print mail (Van Hoof, 1998). Compared to weeks for a response in case of traditional direct marketing messages, e-mail replies may be handled in a couple of hours without too much effort, which enables to adjust the offer or segment for optimum results. Gretzel and Fesenmaier (2001) underline that effective leadership and management plays an important role in achieving effectiveness in IT use. High service quality guarantees advantages like a higher market share, higher profits and lower costs for service providers. In the context of costs, time and quality as central success factors of a service provider, quality management is a permanent task to fulfill customer requirements.

EMPIRICAL STUDY

An empirical study was carried out in a region of the European Alps by sending an e-mail inquiry to the 92 local tourism organizations of the destination. The study's objective was to examine the behavior of local tourism organizations in case of e-mail inquiries by means of mystery guests with regard to response rate, response time and the quality of the response (information breadth) and to reveal potential lacks in knowledge transfer among employees. Many studies were undertaken to test the response behaviour of hotel businesses (Murphy and Tan, 2003; Voss, 2000; Pechlaner et al., 2002). Yet according to the knowledge of the authors, none has examined the response attitude of tourism organizations. The criteria for the assessment of response quality are summarized in Table 1.

Response quality does not solely comprise a prompt response, but an accurate response to the questions asked. Also, the formal aspects like layout, style, attachments etc. have to be met. The chosen research approach should enable to detect differences that explain response behav-

TABLE 1. Evaluated Criteria

Evaluated Criteria
Responsiveness
Average response rate
Average response time
Response time within 12 hours
Information Depth
Response to accommodation request
Response to additional question
Formal Aspects
Number of attachments
Forwarding of inquiries to accommodation providers
Typing mistakes and grammar

ior to internet inquiries. Electronic inquiries were sent via e-mail to a sample of 92 local tourism organizations in an Alpine region over a period of two years. In each season–spring, summer, fall, winter–German, Italian and English e-mail inquiries were sent to the tourism organizations. The e-mail message contained a fictitious accommodation inquiry for a certain period of time. In addition to the accommodation inquiry, the message also included questions concerning other services of the destination (availability of infrastructures in the destination, events taking place at that time, wellness offers in hotels, etc.). The responses of the tourism organizations (e-mail messages) were evaluated with regard to quantity and quality. On the one hand, the number of organizations actually answering to the inquiry was determined. On the other hand, it was of great interest to get to know, how fast the replies arrived and how detailed the inquiries were answered. The size of the tourism organizations with regard to their amount of overnight stays is shown in Table 2.

The outcome of the study is highly important with regard to the internet's increasing significance. The survey shows potential measures that have to be taken on the level of businesses and tourism politics to recognize the significance of the internet for the development of high-quality service processes and its use. Information as a reaction to a potential guest's inquiry represents the first stage of the service process. A stage that is already decisive for the potential customer with regard to his purchase decision and his satisfaction with the service. It must be kept in mind that a well-written and well-structured answer which provides the required information is the first step to win the guest for the respective destination.

Response Behaviour

Response rates correspond to the percentage of answered e-mail requests. Table 3 shows an overview of the response behaviour of the 92

TABLE 2. Size of Tourism Organizations

Size of Tourism Organisations by Overnight Stays		
Category	Frequencies	Percent
0-100,000	56	60.86%
> 100,000	36	39.13%
Total	92	100.00%

TABLE 3. Response Rate (Frequencies)

Response rate				
2004/2005	summer	fall	winter	spring
yes	61	80	89	84
no	31	12	3	8
response rate	66.30%	86.95%	96.73%	91.30%
2003/2004	summer	fall	winter	spring
yes	84	77	74	79
no	8	15	18	13
response rate	91.30%	83.69%	80.43%	85.86%

local tourism organizations over the two-year time period. If both years are compared to each other it is seen that in the first year (2003/2004) fewer e-mails were answered compared to the year 2004/2005. As far as the response rate is concerned, the peak was in winter 2004/2005 with a response of 96.93%.

One major advantage of e-mail inquiries is the speed of information exchange. The time in which an e-mail is answered is crucial in terms of quality. A guest may contact several tourism organizations at the same time at low costs. In the study at hand, response time was measured in hours, whereas the European standard for e-mail responses of tourism organizations lies at a margin of 12 hours. The average response times (in h) over the two-year period amounted to 4 1/2 up to 8 1/4 hours.

As far as the size of the tourism organizations is concerned, the hypothesis is that larger tourism organizations show better response behaviour than smaller ones. They have more employees, more capacities for responding to e-mail inquiries and more opportunities to offer trainings to employees, which likely encourage them to transfer their knowledge to their colleagues. Anyway, the problem of efficient knowledge management for professional e-mail response behaviour (not only in terms of active response but also in terms of detailed information) remains. The results show that those tourism organizations with more than 100,000 overnight stays respond more often than smaller tourism organizations below 100,000 overnight stays.

To sum up, it can be said that the overall response rate of tourism organizations with more than 100,000 overnight stays amounts to 88.89% on average, while smaller tourism organizations (overnight stays < 100,000) respond with 82.81% on average (Figures 4 and 5).

FIGURE 4. Average Response Time

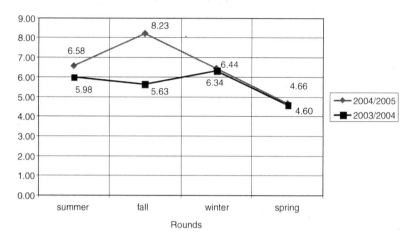

FIGURE 5. Average Response in the Single Period (2003/2004 and 2004/2005) by Category (Overnight Stays)

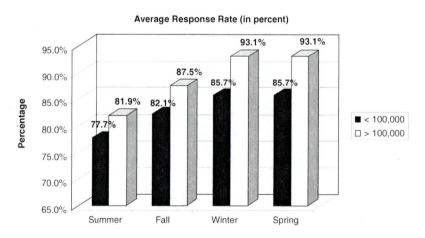

Information Breadth

The main advantage of modern communication media is that customers may access an enormous amount of information at extremely low transaction costs, and may use effective and efficient research tools which enable fast search and decision processes (Hoffmann, Novak and Chatterjee, 1995). Information depth therefore is a crucial dimension of response behavior of tourism organizations. Patch and Smally (1998) also refer to size and contents of e-mail messages as major reasons for possible information overload. The study at hand did not solely ask for accommodation information, but for additional information, for instance riding possibilities, wellness applications, guided mountain tours etc. In terms of information breadth it was assessed if the provided information is accurate, is not accurate or if the questions have not been answered at all.

It becomes apparent that only a small proportion of the surveyed tourism organizations provided an accurate answer to the accommodation inquiry (on average, 36 of the 92 surveyed tourism organizations in 2003/2004 and 27 organizations in 2004/2005 responded correctly). The answers provided in Table 4 for the additional information shows similar results(on average 45 tourism organizations in 2003/2004 and 31 in 2004/2005 answered exactly to the posed questions). It must be kept in mind that inadequate response behaviour might result in a loss of guests for the whole tourism destination. One of the possible reasons for this could be that tourism organizations are confronted with high fluctuation among employees, which likely results in losing a knowledge sharing opportunity.

TABLE 4. Correct Answers on the Inquiries on Accomodation and Additional Information

Breadth of information (accommodation)			
	summer	fall	winter	spring
2003/2004	20	14	63	47
2004/2005	25	20	33	30

Breadth of information (additional information)			
	summer	fall	winter	spring
2003/2004	25	54	41	60
2004/2005	3	47	33	41

When the tourism organizations are grouped in those with overnight stays of more than 100,000 and those with less than 100,000 overnight stays, results show that larger tourism organizations answer the question on the accommodation (e.g., a 3-star hotel providing wellness offers) more precisely than those tourism organizations which are smaller. The only exception which has to be made is in the winter seasons (2003/2004 and 2004/2005) where the tourism organizations with less than 100,000 overnight stays answered the question on accommodation with 57.20% on average, compared to 45.80% of the tourism organizations with more than 100,000 overnight stays (Figure 6).

As far as the additional question is concerned, which was posed with regard to biking, hiking facilities, wellness offers, cultural activities etc. (depending on the season), the outcomes equally reveal that larger tourism organizations on average answer the question more often than smaller ones, exceptionally during the summer and winter survey. For example, in the summer period, 13.90% of the tourism organizations with more than 100,000 overnight stays answered the additional question, compared to 15.20% of tourism organizations with fewer than 100,000 overnight stays (Figure 7).

On the other hand, the growing development of the internet equally changes the purchasing habits of the tourists, for instance, holiday

FIGURE 6. Average Information Breadth (Accommodation) in the Single Periods (2003/2004 and 2004/2005) by Category (Overnight Stays)

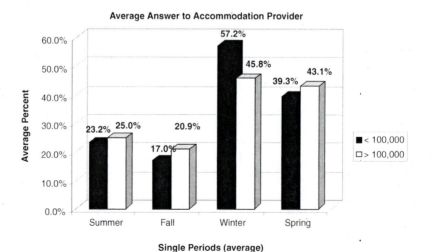

FIGURE 7. Average Information Breadth (Additional Information) in the Single Periods (2003/2004 and 2004/2005) by Category (Overnight Stays)

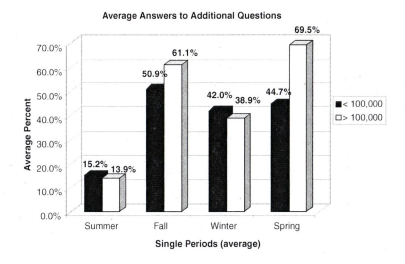

planning and preparation on the computer at home is getting easier. These changes demand big efforts in providing correct and sufficient information to enable a faster decision-making process of the potential guest.

CONCLUDING COMMENTS

There is a long tradition of using mystery guests to examine service standards and determine service quality of businesses in the sector of tourism (Matzler, Pechlaner and Kohl, 2000). In other parts of the service industry the method is known under the name of mystery shopping or silent shopping. Selected observers (mystery guests/mystery shoppers), prepared for the test situation, are acting in a realistic situation as "disguised" customers not to be identified by the employee, in order to assess the quality of services from a customer's point of view by means of an at least partly structured instrument of investigation.

Exploring electronic customer service is a quixotic task. This research primarily explored two aspects of e-mail inquiries, responsiveness and information quality provided to the guest. It must be admitted that neglecting electronic inquiries must be seen as neglecting an opportunity to attract a potential guest to the destination. As already stated, information via internet has gained tremendous importance in the last few years and will become even more important in the future. Yet, it is not only crucial to simply answer an e-mail within an appropriate time, but to provide the required information. In the study at hand, 83.51% of the tourism organizations (in 2003/2004 and 2004/2005) answered the e-mail inquiry of the potential guest, who was asking for accommodation information in the destination, i.e., that 16.49% of the potential guests did not receive information on their inquiry and probably chose another destination for their holidays. The results of the study in terms of general weaknesses in know-how, skills or competencies in the field of quality management, are similar to other existing empirical work (Pechlaner and Fuchs, 2002; Betcherman, McMullen and Davidman, 1998).

Qualitative research could explore why employees of tourism organizations responded as they did, or did not respond at all. One problem that seems to be apparent is that employees in tourism organizations remain for a short period of time resulting in an inefficient knowledge management among employees. Although the regional tourism organization provides training courses for adequate e-mail responding, it seems challenging that one employee hands over his knowledge in answering e-mails to his successor. Another problem is that larger tourism organizations have more money available for training programs and more capacities for responding to e-mail inquiries. This leads to the conclusion that smaller tourism organizations should cooperate or even merge in order to work more professionally and to guarantee a higher quality standard. The merging of several smaller tourism organizations to one big organization would enable efficient quality and knowledge management, could beenfit the realiziaton of competitive advantages and could help attracting potential customers more easily.

FUTURE RESEARCH NEEDS

The main task of local tourism organizations is to answer e-mail inquiries of potential guests and therefore has to be dealt with carefully. Further research will therefore be needed to identify why employees do not answer e-mail inquiries at all or in an unprofessional way, and where and how strongly knowledge transfer lacks. Tourism organizations have to begin to recognize that they play an increasingly important role in knowledge management. It has to be studied how organizations design and deploy approaches to identify, capture, and share information and knowledge so that use and reuse are optimized. The ability to transfer and share practices is an important source of competitive advantage and can lead to the improvement of organizational effectiveness. "Determining which factors promote or impede the sharing of knowledge within groups and organizations constitutes an important area of research" (van den Hoof, de Ridder, 2004, p. 117).

Basically, the problem in tourism organizations seems to be the high fluctuation of employees. The authors believe that tourism organizations have to change their human resource management in terms of training courses being organized as incentives for employees. On the long run, better knowledge sharing would likely be resulting in better service quality and in a higher satisfaction among the employees. With regard to the high fluctuation and apart from training courses, manuals or check lists could be developed within the tourism organization for transfering knwoledge on e-mail responing to new employees. This would improve the information flow and could help to better share knowledge. Another way of benefiting knowledge management could be a system like Wikipedia, which is a free encyclopedia that anyone can edit. This internal posting tool on the subject of e-mail inquiries would benefit the active participation of the single employee which makes him feel relevant for the whole organizations. Employees could add single modules for creating an electronic letter for all kinds of guests' inquiries (e.g., accommodation, theatre program, whatsoever.). Every new employee could then use the Wikipedia for help and further information when he is assigned to respond to e-mail inquiries. Moreover, the organizational commitment of tourism organization employees to their organizations could be enhanced. Wikipedia can be seen as a process which consists of both bringing and getting knowledge. This tool could also be adapted to other issues a tourism organization has to deal with.

In this paper, the authors explored the service quality of online inquiries by potential guests by means of a two-year mystery guest study. The results suggest that both commitment and communication are likely key variables in explaining knowledge sharing. Besides the outcomes of the study itself, some possible reasons for inappropriate e-mail answering by employees have been given and selected tools for increasing knowledge sharing have been presented. Yet, a number of questions have been left unanswered and shall be addressed in the future.

REFERENCES

Anderson, E.W., and Sullivan, M.W. (1993). The antecedents and consequences of customer satisfaction for firms. *Marketing Science*, 12, 125-143.

Betcherman, G., McMullen, K., and Davidman, K. (1998). Training for the New Economy–A Synthesis Report. Canadian Policy Research Networks: Ottawa.

Bieger, T. (1998). Reengineering Destination Marketing Organizations–The Case of Switzerland, 33th TRC-Meeting, 15-18 May, Brijuni.

Bieger, T. (2002). Management von Destinationen. Muenchen/Vienna: Oldenbourg.

Bolinger, A.S., and Smith, R.D. (2001). Managing Organizational Knowledge as a Strategic Asset. *Journal of Knowledge Management*, 5 (1), 8-18.

Buhalis, D., and Licata, M.C. (2002). The Future of E-Tourism Intermediaries. *Tourism Management*, 23 (3), 207-220.

Dunning, J.H. (1993). Multinational Enterprises and the Global Economy. Wokingham/England: Addison Wesley.

Erstad, M. (1998). Mystery Shopping Programmes and Human Resource Management. International *Journal of Contemporary Hospitality Management*, 10 (1), 34-38.

Garvin, D.A. (1984): What does 'Product quality' really mean? *Sloan Management Review*, 26 (1), 25-43.

Gretzel, U., and Fesenmaier D. (2001). Measuring Effective IT Use among American Convention and Visitors Bureaus. In P.J. Sheldon, K.W. Wöber and D.R. Fesenmaier (Eds.), Information and Communication Technologies in Tourism 2001 (pp. 52-61). Vienna/New York: Springer.

Gurteen, D. (1999). Creating a Knowledge Sharing Culture. Retrieved June 3, 2004 from http://www.gurteen.com

Haller, S. (1995). Beurteilung der Dienstleistungsqualitaet. Wiesbaden: Gabler.

Hoffmann D.L., Novak T.P., and P. Chatterjee (1995). Commercial Scenarios for the Web: Opportunities and Challenges. *Journal of Computer Mediated Communication*, 3(3), 1-17.

Kano, N., Seraku, N., Takahashi, F., and Tsuji, S. (1984). Attractive Quality and Must-Be Quality. *The Journal of the Japanese Society for Quality Control*, 14 (2), 39-48.

Malhotra, Y. (2000). Knowledge Management and Virtual Organizations. London: Idea Group Publishing.

Matzler, K., Pechlaner, H., Abfalter D., and Wolf, M. (2005). Determinants of Response to Customer E-mail Inquiries to Hotels: Evidence from Austria. *Tourism Management*, 26, 249-259.

Matzler K., and Hinterhuber H. H. (1998). How to make product development projects more successful by integrating Kano's model of customer satisfaction into Quality Function Deployment, Technovation: The International Journal of Technology and Innovation Management, 18 (1), 25-38.

Murphy, J., and Tan, I. (2003). Journey to Nowhere? E-mail Customer Service by Travel Agents in Singapore. *Tourism Management*, 24, 543-550.

Nonaka, I., and Takeuchi, H. (1995). The Knowledge Creating Company: How Japanese Companies Create the Dynamics of Innovation. New York/Oxford: University Press.

Patch, K., and Smally, E. (1998). E-mail Overload. *Network World*, 16 (43), pp. 1-6.

Pechlaner, H. and Abfalter, D. (2001). Deterritorialization of Tasks and Functions for Alpine Tourism Organizations–The Case of Tyrol. *Turistica*, 9(3/4), pp. 131-145.

Pechlaner, H., Abfalter, D., and Raich, F. (2002). Cross-Border Destination Management Systems in the Alpine Region–The Role of Knowledge Networks on the Example of AlpNet. Journal of Quality Assurance in Hospitality and Tourism, 2002, 3(3/4), pp. 89-107.

Pechlaner, H., and Fuchs,.M. (2002). Towards New Skill Requirements for Destination Organizations–An Exploratory Study. Tourism Analysis, 7 (1), pp. 43-53.

Pechlaner, H., Rienzner, H., Matzler, K., and Osti, L. (2002). Response Attitudes and Behavior of Hotel Industry to Electronic Info Requests. In K.W. Woeber, A.J. Frew and M. Hitz (Eds.), Information and Communication Technologies in Tourism 2002 (pp. 177-186). Vienna/New York: Springer.

Pechlaner, H., and Tschurtschenthaler, P. (2003). Tourism Policy, Tourism Organizations and Change Management in Alpine Regions and Destinations–A European Perspective. Current Issues in Tourism, 6 (6), pp. 508-539.

Rayman-Baccchus, L., and Molina, A. (2001). Internet-Based Tourism Services: Business Issues and Trends. *Futures*, 33 (7), 589-605.

Sigala, M., Airey, D., Jones, P., and A. Lockwood (2001). Investigating the Effect of Multimedia Technologies on the Employment Patterns in Small and Medium Tourism and Hospitality Enterprises in the UK. In P.J. Sheldon, K.W. Woeber and D.R. Fesenmaier (Eds.), Information and Communication Technologies in Tourism 2001 (pp. 201-214). Vienna: Springer.

Smeral, E. (1998). The Impact of Globalization on Small and Medium Enterprises: New Challenges for Tourism Policies in European countries. Tourism Management, 19 (4), pp. 371-380.

Van den Hoof, B., and de Ridder, J.A. (2004). Knowledge Sharing in Conect: The Influence of Organizational Commitment, Communication Climate and CMC Use on Knowledge Sharing. *Journal of Knowledge Management*, 8 (6), 117-130.

Van Hoof, H. (1998). The use of the Internet in the US lodging industry. *FIU Hospitality Review*, 16 (2), 77-90.

Von Krogh, G.F., Ichijo, K., and Nonaka, I. (2000). Enabling Knowledge Creation: How to Unlock the Mystery of Tacit Knowledge and Release the Power of Innovation. New York: Oxford University Press.

Voss, C. (2000). Developing an E-Service Strategy. *Business Strategy Review*, 11 (1), 21-33.

Wei, S., Ruys, H.F., Van Hoof, H.B., and Combrink, T.E. (2001). Uses of the Internet in the Global Hotel Industry. *Journal of Business Research*, 54 (3), 235-241.

Wilson, A.M. (1998). The Role of Mystery Shopping in Service Performance. *Managing Service Quality*, 8 (6), 414-420.

Zeithaml, V.A., Parasuraman, A., and Malhotra, A. (2002). Service Quality Delivery through Web Sites: A Critical Review of Extant Knowledge. *Journal of the Academy of Marketing Science*, 30 (4), 362-375.

doi:10.1300/J162v07n01_04

The Fuchsia Destination Quality Brand:
Low on Quality Assurance,
High on Knowledge Sharing

Megan Woods
Jim Deegan

SUMMARY. Quality has been widely recognised as a source of competitive advantage in tourism (Poon, 1993; Fayos-Sola, 1996; Laws, 2000). Given the shift that has taken place from interfirm competition to interdestination competition (Go and Govers, 2000; Crouch and Ritchie, 1999), a need to focus on the quality management at the destination level has been identified (Laws, 1995 and 2000; Woods, 2003). In an attempt to address this need, a case study of the Fuchsia destination quality brand, West Cork, Ireland, was carried out. The findings revealed that whilst the Fuchsia brand did not appear to function as a powerful signal of quality to the customer, it did provide a support system which fostered an environment conducive to knowledge sharing amongst the tourism service providers applying for brand membership. This was mostly as a result of the policy of compulsory training for brand applicants. The paper reveals the way in which policies and programmes undertaken to

Megan Woods (E-mail: mwoods@shms.com) is MA Programme Manager, SHMS University Centre, Switzerland and Jim Deegan is Director, National Centre for Tourism Policy Studies, University of Limerick, Limerick, Ireland.

[Haworth co-indexing entry note]: "The Fuchsia Destination Quality Brand: Low on Quality Assurance, High on Knowledge Sharing." Woods, Megan, and Jim Deegan. Co-published simultaneously in *Journal of Quality Assurance in Hospitality & Tourism* (The Haworth Hospitality Press, an imprint of The Haworth Press, Inc.) Vol. 7, No. 1/2, 2006, pp. 75-98; and: *Knowledge Sharing and Quality Assurance in Hospitality and Tourism* (ed: Noel Scott and Eric Laws) The Haworth Hospitality Press, an imprint of The Haworth Press, Inc., 2006, pp. 75-98. Single or multiple copies of this article are available for a fee from The Haworth Document Delivery Service [1-800-HAWORTH, 9:00 a.m. - 5:00 p.m. (EST). E-mail address: docdelivery@haworthpress.com].

Available online at http://jqaht.haworthpress.com
© 2006 by The Haworth Press, Inc. All rights reserved.
doi:10.1300/J162v07n01_05

75

overcome reluctance to participate in a destination quality assurance system also helped remove obstacles to knowledge sharing amongst tourism suppliers at the destination. doi:10.1300/J162v07n01_05 *[Article copies available for a fee from The Haworth Document Delivery Service: 1-800-HAWORTH. E-mail address: <docdelivery@haworthpress.com> Website: <http://www.HaworthPress.com> © 2006 by The Haworth Press, Inc. All rights reserved.]*

KEYWORDS. Destination quality brand, knowledge management (KM), knowledge sharing, network, competitiveness, SMTEs

INTRODUCTION

Quality has been widely acknowledged as a source of competitive advantage in tourism (Poon, 1993; Fayos-Sola, 1996; Laws, 2000). As interfirm competition shifts to interdestination competition (Go and Govers, 2000; Crouch and Ritchie, 1999), the importance of managing quality at the destination level is increasingly recognised (Laws, 1995 and 2000; Lenehan and Harrington, 1998; Woods, 2003). Knowledge management (KM) is inextricably linked to quality management and competitiveness (Probst, Raub and Tomhardt, 2000). This paper examines the issues of both quality management and knowledge management at the destination level, by focusing on a rural tourism destination quality brand network, called Fuchsia Brands, based in West Cork, Ireland.

LITERATURE REVIEW

To date, much of the tourism literature on quality has been focused on the agency level, i.e., the level of the individual firm. Laws (2000) concludes his study of the evolution of tourism service quality literature, *'Service Quality in Tourism Research: Are We Walking Tall (Yet)?'* with the implication that service quality management at the destination level constitutes the next phase to be explored. Woods (2003) notes that destination quality management (DQM) is a particularly complex challenge given the compounded service element, the diverse and fragmented nature of the tourism destination and the predominance of small and medium-sized tourism enterprises. It is suggested that any DQM initiative take account of these complexities.

Firstly, given the large number of services at most tourism destinations, the service element, and the challenge it presents, is compounded. Due to service characteristics such as intangibility and inseparability (where consumption takes place during production and under real time conditions), mistakes and shortcomings are harder to conceal. Because services are experiential, they cannot be tested beforehand. The significance of this is that, unlike fast-moving consumer goods (FMCGs), it is not possible to have a trial of the tourism product (Laws, 1995). This increases the risk factor for the consumer. Consequently, any potential to implement a quality assurance system is particularly significant. Whilst there exist a number of quality assurance systems for individual tourism products and services (such as national tourist board approval and various organisational accreditation systems such as AA and RAC), this is not often the case for the destination. Thus, there is a need for some form of destination accreditation system.

Brands offer an alternative to quality assurance systems. 'Branding is a name, term, sign, symbol or design or combination of them, intended to identify the goods or services of one seller or group of sellers and to differentiate them from those of competitors' (Kotler, 2000: 404). Thus, pivotal to the concept of branding is the ability to distinguish one product from amongst its competitors. Indeed, brands are the most obvious source of differentiation for competing products (De Chernatony and McWilliam, 1989). According to Morgan and Pritchard (2002: 21), writing in the specific context of destination branding, 'the point of differentation must reflect a promise which can be delivered and which matches expectations.' Doyle (1998: 174) emphasises the importance of exceeding customer expectations through providing an augmented level of added values, which are 'difficult for competitors to imitate' and a potential level, which builds customer preference and loyalty. Thus, a brand has achieved its 'full potential' when consumers perceive a brand as offering superior brand values and benefits to the competitor offerings, causing them to 'specify' or 'recommend' the brand (Lambkin, Meenagan and O'Dwyer, 1994). Hence, successful brand-building facilitates the brand to act as a differentiating device (Doyle, 1989; Kotler, 2000), a short-hand device in selecting products and services (De Chernatony, 1991), a promise of consistent quality (De Chernatony and McWilliam, 1989), a risk reducer (Kapferer, 2001) and a symbolic device in creating and reinforcing a unique brand image or personality (Kotler, 1988; De Chernatony, 1991). This suggests that if a destination were to develop a brand, it might act as a quality assurance system and thus reduce risk for potential visitors.

The second complexity is the diverse and fragmented nature of the tourism destination product. This characteristic represents a significant challenge for destination mangers in light of the consumer's demand for a quality of experience. Indeed, according to Baum and Henderson (1998: 4):

> One of the biggest challenges facing the delivery of quality in the service sector is represented by the concept of the service delivery chain within which consumers' total experience consists of an amalgam of purchases and non-tariff encounters which may be the delivery management responsibility of a diversity of service providers.

According to Murphy et al. (2000: 44), 'a destination may be viewed as an amalgam of individual products and experience opportunities that combine to form a total experience of the area visited.' This definition underlines how, despite the fragmentation on the supply side, the experience at the destination is perceived as a *gestalt* by the visitor, and that there is a demand on the part of the consumer for a total quality of experience (QOE) (Otto and Ritchie, 1995). This need for coordination and consistency on the supply side is the result of an expectation for such on the demand side. Essentially, today's tourists expect satisfaction with their entire tourist experience at a given local tourism destination rather than merely with the individual components of the total tourism product (e.g., accommodation, catering, activities) that they consume within the destination at different times and places (Ryan, 1997). This suggests that any quality brand should encompass the full gamut of tourism products and services at the destination, in accordance with the concept of multi-product destination branding.

Lastly, the preponderance of small and medium-sized businesses at the tourism destination raises a challenge for destination quality managers. The most commonly found hospitality enterprise is small (Baum, 1999; Morrison and Thomas, 1999; Middleton, 2001). Often, they operate under different constraints than larger firms (Hjalager, 1996; Buhalis and Cooper, 1998; Telfer, 2001; Morrison, 2002). This can have consequences for quality management. Becton and Graetz (2001) in their study of small tourism and hospitality businesses in Australia found that there was a shortage of skilled staff and owner-managers. Those they surveyed had little management training or qualifications. Barriers to further training include the cost of training and inflexibility of hours and place of delivery. This general finding is supported by

Gouirand (1994) who notes in a French tourism context that small hoteliers have neither the time nor the disposition to avail of training. Breiter and Bloomquist (1998: 32) conclude that small and medium-sized hotels are less likely than large hotels to implement TQM: 'The smaller the hotel, the less likely it is to incorporate empowerment, training and development, rewards and recognition, and tools and techniques.' Indeed, Gouirand (1994) states that constraints common to small tourism firms can have serious implications for quality and consumer satisfaction (Gouirand, 1994). Consequently, SMTEs reluctance to engage in quality management may threaten a destination's competitiveness. Thus, any destination quality initiative should aim to include SMTEs.

The complexities of the tourism destination product suggest that a multi-sectoral destination quality brand which caters to SMTEs' needs might prove an effective measure to improve a destination's quality standards and its competitiveness.

Knowledge Management

Knowledge management (KM), along with quality management, has been one of the most dominant concepts in recent years. Both quality management and KM are inextricably linked. From both a practical and theoretical stance, enterprises which fail to deliver quality products and services will not remain competitive in the long term. Knowledge management and sharing have powerful effects on quality, and thus influence important competitive factors (Probst, Raub and Romhardt, 2000). The vast majority of people working in tourism are knowledge workers. It is the combination of their skills and know-how rather than a reliance on physical effort alone, that drives business success. Awad and Ghaziri (2004: 28) define KM as 'the process of gathering and making use of a firm's collective expertise wherever it resides–on paper, in databases or in people's heads,' and knowledge-sharing as 'a process of transferring human knowledge about a process or a procedure to others in the organisation; ability and willingness of people to exchange specialised experience with others for the common good of the organisation.'

In Joseph M. Firestone's foreword to '*The New Knowledge Management: Complexity, Learning and Sustainable Innovation*' (McElroy, 2003), he discusses a number of theories which each offer explanations for the way in which KM is changing. Common to each of these theories is the recognition that KM is a socially driven process as opposed to a technology driven process. As McElroy (2003: 58) himself pithily expresses it, 'It's not always about technology.' KM is fundamentally a social process that can be supported by technology, but that is also susceptible to improvements in its operating dynamics, independent of technology. 'What must come first in the improvement of knowledge production and integration are improvements in the ways people work together to create and to share knowledge' (McElroy, 2003: 58). The link between people and knowledge management is summed up by Allee (2003: 113) as follows:

> Knowledge cannot be separated from the human networks and communities that create it, use it, and transform it. In all types of knowledge work, even where technology is very helpful, people require conversation, experimentation, and experiences shared with other people who do what they do... Our personal knowledge evolves as the conversations we are part of shift and change. Every conversation is an experiment in knowledge creation–testing ideas, trying out words and concepts, continuously creating and re-creating our experience of life itself.

To demonstrate the point, Allee (2003) cites the example of Xerox's technical field representatives documented in the book, '*The Social Life of Information*' (Brown and Duguid: 2000). In the Xerox case study, the system of error codes, intended to facilitate problem identification and resolution in the machine documentation, was found to be inadequate by the representatives. Much more effective problem solving arose from the informal get-togethers during breakfast, coffee breaks and lunches. Interspersed with social activities and gossip, they talked about work continuously. In this way, they kept each other abreast of what they were doing, the problems they were encountering and how they were resolving them. In addition, because of the social ties which built up, they felt comfortable calling on each other for suggestions and advice.

Central to the social aspect of KM is the way tacit knowledge is made explicit. It has been highlighted that given the roots of the concept of tacit knowledge–philosopher Michael Polanyi's (1958) construct of innate intelligence, perception, and capacities for reasoning–it is impossible to make it explicit nor does one need to (Allee, 2003). Tacit and explicit knowledge are two aspects of the one process of knowing: there is no linear progression from one form to the other. However, many researchers' misinterpretation of the Polanyi's tacit knowledge as meaning 'stored memory, experience or content that simply hasn't been articulated' (Allee, 2003: 97) but that allows itself to be extracted, codified and shared with others, has proven a useful construct for examining the area of knowledge sharing. One model which describes the way in which tacit knowledge, as it is often interpreted, is translated into explicit knowledge is Nonaka and Takeuchi's (1995) spiral of knowledge creation. According to Nonaka and Takeuchi, the process of knowing is a social process whereby tacit knowledge–that which is embedded in people's experience–is socialised or shared through direct experience. That shared experience can be articulated into explicit concepts that can then be systemised into a knowledge system. Once systematised, that now-explicit knowledge can be learned by others and once again become embedded in experience as tacit knowledge.

The stages of the knowledge spiral are as follows. Socialisation is the direct conveyance of tacit knowledge through shared experience. Externalisation constitutes the process of articulating tacit knowledge into explicit concepts. Combination is the process of systematising concepts into a knowledge system. Internationalisation represents embodying the explicit knowledge into tacit operational knowledge (Figure 1).

A common myth with regard to KM is that people do not want to share knowledge (Allee, 2003: Awad and Ghaziri, 2004). Allee (2003) dissects this myth maintaining, that people, on the contrary, like to share but refrain from doing so in the face of too many organisational barriers, such as time constraints or a competitive environment where the recognition and reward system are not conducive to the sharing of knowl-

FIGURE 1. Nonaka and Takeuchi's (1995) Knowledge Spiral

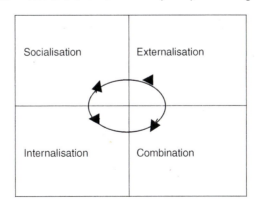

"Figure: Square Matrix with a Spiral Core pg 73," from THE KNOWLEDGE CREATING COMPANY: HOW JAPANESE COMPANIES CREATE THE DYNAMICS OF INNOVATION by Ikujiro Nonaka and Hirotaka Takeuchi, copyright Oxford University Press, Ltd. Used by permission of Oxford University Press, Inc.

edge. Awad and Ghaziri (2004) qualify this with the observation that the willingness to share depends on the attitude of the knower, who the requester is, company culture, sensitivity of the knowledge requested, availability of attractive motivators, and trust level among company personnel. Consensus reigns with regard to the challenge facing management. It is management's task to foster an environment and implement a system conducive to the sharing of knowledge. In order to facilitate sharing, the business must instill trust within the business, and give employees and management an opportunity to forge solid relationships founded on trust (Allee, 2003; Awad and Ghaziri, 2004).

The Task of Managing Knowledge

With regard to both KM theory and practice it is useful to distinguish between knowledge management and knowledge processing. This distinction is central to McElroy's (2003) 'new KM' or 'second generation KM' (Figure 2). Knowledge management is a management activity that seeks to enhance knowledge processing. Knowledge processing is a set of social processes through which people in organisations create and integrate their knowledge. Knowledge processing is made up of two components, namely knowledge production and integration (McElroy, 2003). Knowledge production relates to the creation of knowledge, whilst knowledge integration concerns the sharing of knowledge.

In the 'new' or 'second generation' KM, knowledge processing is not only a social process but a self-organising one as well, where certain behaviours automatically emerge (McElroy, 2003). Whilst, this essentially suggests that no management is required, there is a need,

FIGURE 2. The Processes of McElroy's (2003) Second Generation KM

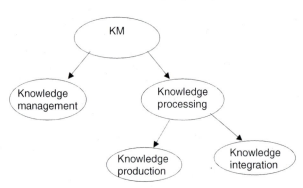

nonetheless, for policies and programmes to support, strengthen and reinforce those behaviours. Consequently, the management task is to *set* the conditions for emergent knowledge processing as opposed to *designing* them. 'The focus is therefore on creating an appropriate organisational culture and providing effective leadership' (Kermally, 2002: 1) that facilitates the creation, transfer and sharing of knowledge. The goal is to allow access to scarce resources, new insights, new expertise, cross fertilisation of knowledge and to promote and facilitate knowledge sharing, collaboration and networking. Collaboration means the ability to connect diverse assets into unique capabilities in pursuit of new opportunities for personal, group, and organisational growth (Awad and Ghaziri, 2004). To create an appropriate organisational culture, managers need to implement policies and programmes that make it possible for the social knowledge processing systems to be ideally structured (McElroy, 2003). The literature on adaptive systems theory (e.g., Stacy, 1996) suggests that high rates of diversity in membership, extensive interactions between agents, and the presence of groups or communities constitute the ideal structure with regard to creativity and adaptivity. This indicates that a multi-sectoral network of suppliers at a tourism destination could lend itself well to knowledge sharing. The task for the destination managers would be to foster a culture conducive to knowledge sharing across a network.

Value Networks and Communities of Practice

According to Allee (2003: 14), 'the network is the most natural and powerful thing for creating and sharing knowledge.' Knowledge networks and business networks are sets of informal relationships in which connections are always shifting and changing. The primary focus of informal networks is to collect and pass along information. There is no joint enterprise that holds them together, such as the development of shared tools' (Allee, 2003: 115). They are merely a set of relationships. In contrast, practice communities have stronger ties and more deliberate relationships than knowledge networks (Allee, 2003). Members are keen to learn from each other and discover ways to create events or projects which will help all involved to improve their knowledge and skills. They may share tools, methods and tips and may even have a systematic way of collecting these. As a result, a strong sense of community evolves. 'Membership is usually self-selecting and people are held together by passion and commitment. Practice communities require a sense of mission–there is something people want to accomplish or do together that arises from their shared understanding' (Allee, 2003: 116). To be considered a real community of practice the three following elements must be present (Wenger, McDermott and Snyder, 2002):

- Domain (what they know). People organise around a domain of knowledge that gives members a sense of joint enterprise and brings them together. Members identify with the domain of knowledge and a joint undertaking that emerges from a shared understanding of their situation.
- Community (who they are). People function as a community through relationships of mutual engagement that bind members together in a social entity. They interact regularly and engage in joint activities that build relationships and trust.
- Practice (what they do). The community builds capability in practice by developing shared repertoires and resources (tools, documents, routines, vocabulary, symbols, artefacts, etc.) that embody the accumulated knowledge of the community. This accumulated knowledge serves as a foundation for future learning.

Allee (2003) maintains that the trend is towards building not simply working relationships, but also human relationships that build trust and open the channels for knowledge sharing and creativity. Whilst McElroy (2003) maintains that the managers must set the conditions for this rather than design them, Wenger, McDermott and Snyder (2002) outline a number of specific management roles which management must undertake in order to achieve this in the context of a practice community or value network. These roles may vary in accordance with value network life cycle and may include:

- Staging an awareness campaign and identifying the benefits of practice communities;
- Facilitating participants to find common ground through group dialogue;
- Identifying what knowledge a community wants or needs to share;
- Facilitating dialogue around identity and joint enterprise;
- Designing, facilitating and documenting informal meetings;
- Designing and creating a community support structure;
- Guiding a community through growth;
- Co-developing support strategies for the group learning agenda;
- Creating frameworks, guidelines, measures and reality checks for development;

- Working with the community on commitment and sustaining energy; and
- Addressing organisational issues that may be helping or hindering activity.

The findings of this paper relate to the ways in which the management of a network, founded as a destination quality assurance system, was effective in cultivating an ideal environment for knowledge sharing amongst tourism suppliers at the destination. Before presenting these, the methodology is discussed.

METHODOLOGY

To arrive at a greater understanding of the effectiveness of a regional destination quality brand as a quality assurance system, and of the dynamics of KM within that system, an evaluative case study approach was used. A criteria-based procedure was used to select the case study. The criteria included the following attributes: recognition as a destination quality initiative; a certain number of brand members representing different tourism activities; a composition of mostly small tourism enterprises; and the potential for networking amongst its members. The Fuchsia brand was considered to fulfil these criteria, insofar as it was Ireland's first local destination quality brand, and since its inception has gained widespread recognition as a successful tourism training and networking initiative. Established following the success of a similar food network, the tourism network encompasses a wide variety of tourism service enterprises from the accommodation, restaurant, transport, activity and visitor attraction sectors, and had a total of 64 brand members at the time of investigation. The businesses are mostly micro in size, and often family-run. With regard to the destination itself, West Cork is situated in the south western corner of Ireland. The area is famed for the richness and diversity of its heritage, culture and landscape. The region's attractions range from the town of Kinsale in the east, which is known as the gourmet capital of Ireland, to a series of rugged peninsulas in the west jutting into the Atlantic Ocean. Other attractions include bustling market towns, heritage and archaeological sites, stretches of sandy beach, and opportunities for golfing, sailing, diving and hiking.

The main methodology employed was a series of in-depth face-to-face interviews with brand managers and brand members. The total number of tourism service providers willing and available to be interviewed totalled 46 out of 64, accounting for 58 of the 78 establishments which belong to the brand. The 46 interviews covered establishments in the following categories: hotels, guesthouses, self-catering accommodation, bed and breakfasts, hostels, caravan and camp-sites, restaurants, activities (such as diving, sailing and walking), attractions (such as a model railway village, heritage centre, parks and gardens) and transport (island ferry), and as such included every enterprise type represented in the brand. The interviews were carried out during the winter of 2002, and were conducted on the premises of each interviewee.

In order to gain an insight into the effectiveness of the quality brand, respondents were asked to discuss different aspects of brand membership during the in-depth interviews. These included *inter alia* motivations for joining, the advantages and drawbacks of brand membership, the relevance and fruitfulness of the membership criteria, and the nature of any links each enterprise had with other tourism enterprises, be they brand members or not. In all cases, the most directly involved and knowledgeable individual within each enterprise was interviewed. These were either the owners/managers of the businesses and/or those who had participated in the training courses (the completion of which is an important prerequisite for attaining brand membership). All interviews were recorded and transcribed word for word for subsequent analysis.

FINDINGS

It became clear from interviews with the brand members that the Fuchsia brand did not appear to function as an effective quality assurance signal to potential visitors. Pivotal to the concept of branding is the function of differentiation. Indeed, brands are the most obvious source of differentiation for competing products (De Chernatony and McWilliam, 1989). It follows that, for the brand to be successful in differentiating a product or service from its competitor, it is essential that the message emitted by the brand is received by the consumers. As Duncan and Moriarty (1997: 9) remark, 'Brands exists in the stakeholders' heads and hearts, not just on the sides of packages.' The findings revealed that the Fuchsia brand did not fulfil such a role for visitors to the destination. Brand members spoke of their experience with visitors and guests and recounted how they often had to explain what the Fuchsia logo symbolised. There was no evidence to suggest that the brand represented a promised which had been made to visitors against which expectations could be matched, in the way that Morgan and Pritchard (2002) underline a destination brand should. Some members felt it would be a question of time before brand recognition was achieved, whilst others felt that the other advantages such as joint marketing, access to subsidised training, and advice and guidance compensated for this lack of recognition. A major weakness of the network's quality assurance system was the perceived lack of effective quality monitoring system. Whilst training did play a role in the suppliers' perception of the brand's effectiveness, monitoring of quality was seen to be the predominant determinant of brand members' confidence in the quality brand. This is in keeping with the emphasis on quality control present in other quality models such as ISO 9000, EFQM, Deming and Baldrige, and supports much of the quality literature. In this case study, the quality monitoring system in place, which comprised of approval by the national tourist board and feedback from customer response cards, was deemed to be ineffective. The majority of members felt that a more satisfactory quality monitoring system involving independent audits, regular on-site inspections and mystery visits would need to be implemented to ensure 'the long-term well-being of the brand.' However, most were content to continue their association with the brand organisation given that it was a community project heavily financed by European Union funding. Nonetheless, in light of the pending cessation of EU funding, and the consequent introduction of a membership fee, a number of brand members felt that the brand would be threatened by competition from other quality assurance organisations whose logos constituted stronger and more effective signals to potential visitors. In this sense, the Fuchsia brand was not conceived as a powerful destination brand.

Overcoming Barriers

Whilst the findings indicated that the brand did not function as a quality assurance signal to the potential visitor, it was found, however, that the policies and programmes which created a climate conducive to the participation of local tourism service suppliers in the quality assurance initiative also helped cultivate an environment which lent itself to effective knowledge sharing, and that this reaped benefits for members of the destination network. Essentially, in overcoming the barriers to participation in a destination quality assurance system, the obstacles to knowledge sharing amongst local tourism suppliers were also overcome. The main obstacles to training for small tourism businesses are lack of time, venue and finance (Becton and Graetz, 2001). The key inhibitors of knowledge transfer are lack of trust, lack of time and conference venues, status of the knower, and quality and speed of transfer. 'Each inhibitor should be seriously considered before knowledge transfer can be expected to take hold reliably among participants' (Awad and Ghaziri, 2004: 275). The way in which the Fuchsia brand management's policies and programmes is the focus of this paper.

The challenge with which Fuchsia's brand management was faced was no easy one as was evidenced by the members' responses. A lack of trust and the presence of a competitive and territorial mentality were found in West Cork, the destination under investigation in this case study. One respondent, a Bed & Breakfast (B&B) owner (less than five employees), described the distrustful and competitive spirit with which the local B&B community greeted her when she first set up her business.

> Tourism is a kind of a cut-throat business, it's like a new member is looked upon as 'taking all our guests,' not as, 'great, a new member is here.' It doesn't work like that. When I was opening up here and looking for advice from the other B&Bs, they all said, forget it, there wasn't a penny to be made in it. . . The thing about B&Bs is, they're hostile to newcomers. . .

This distrust and fear of competition appeared to be common, not just to B & Bs, but to other sectors too. Another respondent, the owner of a diving school (less than five employees), spoke of her vain attempts to work together with another diving school in the area. In trying to understand their 'insular' logic, she supposed that the others were:

> . . . frightened that you might know what they're up to or what they're doing. . . I don't know, maybe it's early days here yet, and they feel they've only just got going, and it's been a lot of hard work and they feel, 'I don't want to share that knowledge or success with anyone else.' You look at garages. You get one garage and then you get five garages because they all work well and people know. That's not happening in activities yet.

These testimonies highlight the challenge of increasing the level of participation and co-operation amongst tourism service providers at the destination and support the general observation that small independent firms tend to be reluctant to co-operate (Gouirand, 1994; Sablerie, 1996; Luciani, 1999; Synergy, 2000).

In the context of tourism collaboration, the need for a referent organisation is underlined (Jamal and Getz, 1995). With specific regard to a collaborative quality initiative, Augustyn (2001) concludes that there is a need for a formal organisation to guarantee success. In the literature review on knowledge management and value chains, the importance of creating trust and facilitating collaboration is underlined (Allee, 2003; Awad and Ghaziri, 2004). During the interviews, regular reference was made to the role played by the management of Fuchsia Brands. Expressions such as 'where Fuchsia comes into it. . . ' and 'Fuchsia would've made me aware of it' were common. The comment made by an owner of a caravan and camp-site (less than five employees) is representative of the members' references to the role which Fuchsia Brands played in converting a potentially insular mentality to a more open spirit where knowledge sharing could flourish.

> We all shared our ideas, and we all shared different aspects of the course, and then it was just that Fuchsia Brands brought us together. . . and not that we'd be prejudiced against anybody else, but usually people keep their ideas to themselves. The Fuchsia Brand brought us altogether and made us realise the power of networking.

It is clear from the findings that Fuchsia management's policies and programmes established as pillars of the quality management system played a critical role to setting the conditions for knowledge sharing.

Training: A Critical Policy

One policy which was considered to be critical to quality management at the destination level was the criterion of compulsory participation in training for those who wished to become members of the brand. This training played a pivotal role in raising the level of quality in the individual firm as well as conveying to other members that certain standards had been passed. Management organised the training courses so that they would remove barriers to further training for small tourism businesses including 'the cost of training and inflexibility of hours and place of delivery' (Becton and Graetz, 2001: 113). One respondent, a self-catering operator (less than five employees), summed up the sentiment of many members, when he commented, 'they've given everyone who's joined every chance of doing the courses and learning.'

With regard to place of delivery, training courses were held locally throughout the region, with specific venues varying between different towns so as to share the onus of travelling amongst the applicants. Although some interviewees found that the journey time and distance to the training venue were prohibitive, others appreciated that the alternative would have been to travel to the major cities of Cork or Dublin. The latter situation was seen to be a major deterrent, and the difference made, especially to small and family businesses, in having training courses that were 'local' and 'convenient' was expressed as follows by a B & B owner: 'Oh, they [the brand members] wouldn't have done it otherwise! One hundred per cent wouldn't have done it because you couldn't do it! Oh, bringing the training to us was one of the best things they ever did.' Thus, the obstacle of venue for knowledge sharing was overcome.

Similarly, brand membership helped overcome time restraints. With regard to the convenience of timing of the training courses, expressions like 'they didn't take too long' and 'they're run over winter' were commonly used. In light of Fyall et al.'s (2001) observation that the urge to collaborate appears more pressing in the shoulder and off-peak periods of the tourist season, when visitor numbers are at their lowest, it was fitting that training was organised for these periods, lessening the inconvenience for tourism service providers.

Sabel (1992), Jamal and Getz (1995), Selin and Chavez (1995) and Bramwell and Sharman (1999) underline the necessity of incentives, rewards and the recognition of individual and/or mutual benefits for stakeholders' participation to be enhanced. The incentive for bringing the destination's tourism service providers together was that training courses were heavily subsidised. Several operators mentioned that if an operator wanted to undertake the training independently without the support of the brand, that it 'would cost you a fortune,' i.e. that the cost would be prohibitive. Thus, the barrier to knowledge sharing of cost (Allee, 2003) was overcome.

The general feedback concerning the training was that most of the courses were tailored to small tourism business in terms of timing, venue, required investment, content style and delivery. Thus, within the destination quality network framework, a support infrastructure was provided to overcome the typical obstacles common to small businesses, and to encourage involvement in a quality network. In overcoming the obstacles to participation in training, the management similarly directly overcame a number of the key inhibitors to knowledge sharing, such as lack of time and conference places. The facilitated training was crucial insofar as it constituted the primary opportunity for face-to-face contact between the tourism suppliers. This essentially provided a forum for networking for SMTEs, which allowed the self-emergent behavioural patterns of knowledge processing to emerge (McElroy, 2003).

In addition to lack of time and conference places, McElroy identifies the status of the knower and of the enquirer as further obstacles to KM. The training brought the brand applicants together in an informal context without hierarchies, where participants tended to see each other as equals with a common goal. Many in the area of West Cork, traditionally dependent on agriculture or mariculture, were new to the tourism and hospitality industry. For these newly-established and often small businesses, the sense of solidarity, of 'knowing you're not alone,' but part of a network was comforting and reassuring. Thus, as important to some operators as the newly acquired skills themselves, was the feeling of solidarity with other brand members, regardless of sector, which arose out of the exchanges. One manager of an activity centre and self-catering accommodation (less than five employees), a newcomer to the area with a newly established business, conveyed the importance of being in a network of like-minded people in similar situations:

> It's nice to meet everyone else who's involved and I think that's been the big plus actually, meeting people just like me and my husband. . . They've set up their own business and we're all in it together if you like, we're all struggling, we're all trying to get something off the ground, so that was the most interesting thing to meet the people who were setting up a B&B on the Beara peninsula, and the lady doing the garden trail, just to talk to them and see how they were getting on.

This is reminiscent of Wenger et al.'s (2002) element of 'domain' (what they know): one of the three necessary elements to be considered a community of practice. This shared understanding of their situation seemed to partly contribute to a general spirit of co-operation amongst these members, many of whom were theoretically in competition with each other. Many spoke unprompted of the benefits of networking and felt that there was a real ethos of co-operation and indeed, at this tourism destination, a spirit of 'community.' The function of the quality network as 'social glue' (Porter, 1998) was expressed by one manager of an activity centre (less than five employees) as follows:

> And I think what's it's done is to have made a community that are working *together* as opposed to *against* each other. And if you get to know people and you've met the people down the road doing B&B, they're not just competition, so you get on. Because you know the people, you don't treat them as competition.

This clearly echoes Wenger et al.'s (2002) construct of community (who they are), the second element of a community of practice. It is evident from the above quote that the face to face contact in an informal environment between tourism suppliers allowed them to identify similar experiences and for the barriers between 'knowers' and 'requesters' so that trust could be built and knowledge flow more freely.

The removal of the above obstacles to knowledge sharing appeared to have an impact on quality and speed of knowledge transfer. Due to the informal nature of the training, which allowed for direct interaction between tourism service providers with common concerns, shared experiences and a sense of community, there was much scope for knowledge exchange within the network. Regardless of sector, many businesses, including the larger and long-established businesses, but in particular the SMTES and the newly established firms, commented that they had learned as much from talking to other brand applicants as from listening to the trainers. As one B & B owner (less than five employees) typically commented:

> You learn from the people giving the courses but you learn as much from the people doing them as well because there's nothing like experience. If you meet up with people from your own sector which is B&B, and see how they handle situations. . . and I mean, I was new and you're speaking to someone with ten years in the B&B business, and if you find out how they'd handle a certain situation, well, if it works for them, it might work for me also.

This live knowledge exchange occurred across sectors as well as within sectors, as a hotel manager (more than 50 employees) testified.

> I know that if I go to different meetings, when I meet someone it's amazing, some questions come up, and some information that I might have come across or they might have come across–they might be a different type of premises like a visitor attraction or guesthouse accommodation or whatever–and just looking at things from differ-

ent angles, you're always learning, and it's just creating that network in that sense of exchanging information and ideas.

This supports Morrison's (2003) emphasis on the effectiveness of peer-learning, acknowledging that owner-managers may have a certain respect for each other (Wyer, Mason and Theodorakopoulos, 2000). In addition, the findings support Kermally's (2002) thesis that KM does not discriminate as far as the size or sector of the enterprise is concerned.

Policies and Programmes . . . and Personalities

McElroy (2003) maintains that it is the role of management to set the conditions for self-emerging behaviour conducive to knowledge sharing, and that this is to be achieved through appropriate programmes and policies. It is clear from the findings that the policy of compulsory participation in training programmes, which resulted in direct physical interaction amongst a number of providers of diverse tourism offerings, was instrumental in the development of trust, which in turn led to significant knowledge sharing. In addition, it was widely recognised that the brand organisation had played an important intermediary role in breaking down the traditional barriers and creating an atmosphere of trust, where none had existed before, in a manner reminiscent of the 'honest broker' of the Industrial District and network literature (Chaston, 1996; Arzeni and Pellegrin, 1997) or 'convenor,' as Palmer and Bejou (1995) term it. The Fuchsia management undertook many of the roles identified by Wenger et al. (2002) such as staging awareness campaigns, facilitating dialogue around identity and joint enterprise, and working with the community on commitment and sustaining energy.

The findings reveal that in addition to the respective policies and programmes, approaches and personalities of the individual brand managers played a significant role in facilitating knowledge sharing. Many referred to the main individuals involved, citing examples of the ways in which they had been helpful and ready with advice. There was a general consensus that the brand managers were 'professional,' 'business-like' and 'seemed to know what they were at.' This highlights the importance of expertise, legitimacy and authority (Jamal and Getz, 1995; Palmer and Bejou, 1995) in the brokership role and suggests that sufficient expertise and professionalism on the part of the brand managers is crucial in creating an environment conducive to knowledge sharing. Whilst personal relationships between brand members were important for trust building, so too were personal relationships between the brand members and the brand managers. One hotelier's observation was typical: 'Jean O'Sullivan [one of the destination brand managers] would be very much at the core and getting everybody together and encouraging you to support other people and other things.' This suggests that enthusiasm is a further necessary trait for successful knowledge managers. Thus, in addition to the actual functions and their professional execution by brand management, a large part of the Fuchsia Brands' success in this guiding and supportive role appeared to lie with the personalities responsible for managing the brand. The particular words 'approachable' and 'approachability' were often used by the interviewees to describe the brand managers. As one hostel owner (less than five employees) noted:

> Jean is very good for keeping us all in touch. She has us on the e-mail, and keeps us informed of everything that happens or is going to happen. She often just e-mails to see what we think of this or that, or whether there is anything that we would like to do. You know you can say it to her. She is very approachable. And she's so down to earth, and that makes it easier.

The importance of personalities underlines that KM is concerned with social processes.

CONCLUSION

At the time the researcher was carrying out the case study, many members maintained that they would be willing to pay a network membership fee, which was about to be introduced (and since has been). It appears that members would not have been prepared to pay a fee at the outset, but membership had shown them the advantages of belonging to a quality network. Many of these advantages related not to effective quality assurance for the consumer, but to the knowledge sharing which had taken place within the network. This highlights firstly the power that KM can have as a means of keeping members involved in a quality network, and supports Selin and Chavez's (1995) emphasis on the 'programmatic' outcomes, or as Haywood (1997), writing in the specific context of quality management at the destination level, terms it, 'something visible and concrete.' Secondly, the findings highlight the role that KM plays in improving the quality of tourism services within a network.

The emphasis of this paper was on management's task of creating an environment conducive to the social process of knowledge sharing. Whilst there was ample evidence of knowledge sharing, there was less so of knowledge capture. The Fuchsia network needs to look at making explicit knowledge tacit, in other words, embedding the shared knowledge and experience back into the organisation in order that it can be availed of in the future, i.e., so that it can be shared in a formal manner and reused (Turban and Aronson, 2001). To use the terminology of Nonaka and Takeuchi's knowledge spiral, the Fuchsia Brand, having successfully provided the appropriate climate for socialisation and externalisation, need to design policies and programmes to help facilitate the phases of combination and internalisation. This suggests that a future focus should lie on knowledge capture and the use of technology to support a system which enables the knowledge, once it has been shared to become embedded in the organisation, and thus passed on to future generations of members. As Pyo (2005: 583) claims, 'capturing and subsequent dissemination of knowledge at an appropriate time to the individual who needs it with less search cost is the essence of knowledge management.' Fuchsia brands need to be more systematic about designing policies and programmes that govern the other elements of KM such as knowledge capture and dissemination, or for example–destination knowledge maps should be prepared before establishing destination KM systems so that knowledge extraction, classification and organisation processes can be based on the destination knowledge map (Pyo, 2005). Lastly, this paper supports existing literature which underlines the link between quality management and knowledge. It was shown that the barriers to both at the tourism destination are similar, that similar frameworks help overcome those obstacles that in overcoming the obstacles, and that as both quality management and knowledge management systems feed into one another.

REFERENCES

Allee, V., 2003. *The Future of Knowledge: Increasing Prosperity through Value Networks*. Oxford: Butterworth-Heinemann.

Augustyn, M.M., 2001. "Can Local Tourism Destinations Benefit from Employing the ISO 9000:2000 Quality Management System?" In: *Tourism, Innovation and Regional Development: Proceedings of the ATLAS 10th Anniversary Conference*, Dublin, October 4-6. Dublin: ATLAS.

Awad, E.M. and Ghaziri, H.M., 2004. *Knowledge Management*. Upper Saddle River, New Jersey: Pearson Education, Inc.

Baum, T., 1999. Human Resource Management in Tourism's Small Business Sector: Policy Dimensions. In: D. Lee-Ross (Ed), *HRM in Tourism and Hospitality: International Perspectives on Small to Medium-Sized Firms*. London: Cassell, 3-16.

Baum, T. and J. Henderson, 1998. "Quality Enhancement as a Key to Competitiveness–the Case of Singapore." In: *Proceedings of the EuroCHRIE Conference on Competitiveness in the International Hospitality Industry*, Lausanne, Switzerland, November 5-6, 1998.

Becton, S. and B. Graetz, 2001. "Small Business–Small Minded? Training Attitudes and Needs of the Tourism and Hospitality Industry." *International Journal of Tourism Research.*, 3, 105-113.

Bramwell, B. and A. Sharman, 1999. "Collaboration in Local Tourism Policymaking." *Annals of Tourism Research.*, 26(2), 392-415.

Breiter, D. and P. Bloomquist, 1998. "TQM in American Hotels: An Analysis of Application." *Cornell Hotel and Restaurant Administration Quarterly.*, 39(1), Feb, 26-33.

Brown, J.S. and P. Duguid, 2000. The Social Life of Information. Harvard Business School Press, 2000.

Buhalis, D. and C. Cooper, 1998. Competition or Co-operation? Small and Medium-Sized Tourism Enterprises at the Destination. In: E. Laws, H.W. Faulkner, and G. Moscardo (Eds), *Embracing and Managing Change in Tourism: International Case Studies*. London: Routledge, 324-346.

Crouch G.I. and J.R.B. Ritchie, 1999. "Tourism, Competitiveness, and Societal Prosperity." *Journal of Business Research.*, 44, 137-152.

De Chernatony, L., 1991. "Formulating Brand Strategy." *European Management Journal.*, 9(2), 194-200.

De Chernatony, L. and G. McWilliam, 1989. "The Strategic Implications of Clarifying How Marketers Interpret Brands." *Journal of Marketing Management.*, 5(2), 77-95.

Doyle, P., 1989. "Building Successful Brands: The Strategic Options." *Journal of Marketing Management.*, 5(1), 77-95.

Doyle, P., 1998. *Marketing Management and Strategy*. 2nd ed. London: Prentice Hall.

Duncan, T. and S. Moriarty, 1997. *Driving Brand Value Using Integrated Marketing to Manage Profitable Stakeholder Relationships*. Oxford: Blackwell Publishers.

Fayos-Solá, E., 1996. "Tourism Policy: A Midsummer Night's Dream?" *Tourism Management.*, 17(6), 405-412.

Go, F.S., and R. Govers, 2000. "Integrated Quality Management for Tourist Destinations: A European Perspective on Achieving Competitiveness." *Tourism Management.*, 21(1), 79-88.

Gouirand, P., 1994. "La Formation à la Gestion et à la Qualité dans l'Hôtellerie Familiale et Indépendante." In: *WTO Seminar on Quality–A Challenge for Tourism.*, Madrid, 18-19 April, 1994. Madrid: WTO, 91-95.

Hjalager, A., 1996. "Agricultural Diversification into Tourism: Evidence of a European Community Development Program." *Tourism Management.*, 17(2), 103-111.

Jamal, T.B. and D. Getz, 1995. "Collaboration Theory and Community Tourism Planning." *Annals of Tourism Research.*, 22(1), 186-204.

Kapferer, J., 2001. *Reinventing the Brand*. London: Kogan Page.

Kermally, S., 2002. *Effective Knowledge Management: A Best Practice Blueprint*. Chichester: Wiley.

Kotler, P., 2000. *Marketing Management*. The Millennium Edition. New Jersey: Prentice Hall.

Lambkin, M., T. Meenaghan and M. O'Dwyer, 1994. International Brand Strategy: Its Relevance for Irish Marketing. In (Eds) M. Lambkin and T. Meenaghan, *Perspectives on Marketing Management in Ireland*. Dublin: Oak Tree Press, 167-185.

Laws, E., 1995. *Tourism Destination Management: Issues, Analysis and Policies*. London: Routledge.

Laws, E., 2000. "Service Quality in Tourism Research: Are We Walking Tall (Yet)?" *Journal of Quality Assurance in Hospitality and Tourism.*, 1(1), 31-56.

Lenehan, T. and D. Harrington, 1998. *Managing Quality in Tourism: Theory and Practice*. Dublin: Oak Tree Press.

McElroy, M.W., 2003. The New Knowledge Management Complexity: Learning and Sustainable Innovation. Butterworth-Heinemann, London.

Middleton, V., 2001. *Marketing in Travel and Tourism*. Oxford: Butterworth-Heinemann.

Morgan, N. and A. Pritchard, 2002. Contextualising Destination Branding. In: N. Morgan, A. Prichard and R. Pride (Eds), *Destination Branding: Creating the Unique Destination Proposition*. Oxford: Butterworth-Heinemann. 11-41.

Morrison, A.J. and R. Thomas, 1999. "The Future of Small Firms in the Hospitality Industry." *International Journal of Contemporary Hospitality Management.*, 11(4), 148-154.

Morrison, A.J., 2002. "The Small Hospitality Business: Enduring or Endangered?" *Journal of Hospitality and Tourism Management.*, 9(1), 1-11.

Morrison, A.J., 2003. "SME Management and Leadership Development: Market Reorientation." *Journal of Management Development.*, 22(9), 796-808.

Murphy, P., M.P. Pritchard and B. Smith, 2000. "The Destination Product and its Impact on Traveller Perceptions." *Tourism Management.*, 21(1) February, 43-52.

Nonaka, I. and H. Takeuchi, 1995. The Knowledge Creating Company: How Japanese Companies Create the Dynamics of Innovation. Oxford: Oxford University Press.

Otto, J.E. and J.R.B. Ritchie, 1995. "Exploring the Quality of the Service Experience: A Theoretical and Empirical Analysis." *Advances in Services Marketing and Management.*, 5, 37-63.

Polanyi, M., 1958. Personal Knowlegde: Towards a Post-Critical Philosophy. London: Routledge.

Probst, G., S. Raub and K. Romhardt, 2000. Managing Knowledge: Building Blocks for Success. Chichester: Wiley.

Ryan, C., 1997. *The Tourist Experience: A New Introduction*. London: Cassell.

Sabel, C.F., 1992. Studied Trust: Building New Forms of Co-operation in a Volatile Economy. In: F. Pyke and W. Sengenberger (Eds), *Industrial Districts and Local Economic Regeneration*. Geneva, International Labour Organisation, 215-250.

Selin, S. and D. Chavez, 1995. "Developing an Evolutionary Tourism Partnership Model." *Annals of Tourism Research.*, 22(4), 844-856.

Stacy, R.D., 1996. Complexity and Creativity in Organisations. San Francisco: Berrett-Koehler, 1996.

Telfer, D.J, 2001. "Strategic Alliances Along the Niagara Wine Route." *Tourism Management.*, 22(1), 21-30.

Turban, E. and J.E. Aronson, 2000. *Decision Support Systems and Intelligent Systems* (6th ed.) Englewood Cliffs, NJ: Prentice-Hall.

Wenger, E., R. McDermott and W.M. Snyder, 2002. *Cultivating Communities of Practice: A Guide to Managing Knowledge.* Boston, MA: Harvard Business School Press.

Woods, M. and J. Deegan, 2003. "A Warm Welcome for Destination Quality Brands: the Example of the Pays Cathare Region." *International Journal of Tourism Research.* 5, 269-282.

Wyer, P., J. Mason and N. Theodorakopoulos, 2000. "Small Business Development and the 'Learning Organisation'." *International Journal of Entrepreneurial Behaviour and Research.*, 6(4), 239-259.

doi:10.1300/J162v07n01_05

Understanding and Sharing Knowledge of New Tourism Markets: The Example of Australia's Inbound Chinese Tourism

Grace W. Pan
Noel Scott
Eric Laws

SUMMARY. This paper examines issues involved in the definition, creation, and use of knowledge about the Chinese outbound market. It provides an initial view of the type of knowledge required by tourism managers in Australia, some suggestions about where this knowledge is available, or how it may be produced, and identifies issues in sharing that knowledge between tourism industry members and between academics and the industry. doi:10.1300/J162v07n01_06 *[Article copies available for a fee from The Haworth Document Delivery Service: 1-800-HAWORTH. E-mail address: <docdelivery@haworthpress.com> Website: <http://www.HaworthPress. com> © 2006 by The Haworth Press, Inc. All rights reserved.]*

Grace W. Pan is Lecturer, Department of Tourism, Leisure, Hotel and Sport Management, Services Industry Research Centre, Griffith University, Gold Coast, Queensland Australia (E-mail: G.WenPan@griffith.edu.au). Noel Scott is Lecturer, School of Tourism and Leisure Management, University of Queensland, Ipswich Campus, 11 Salisbury Road, Ipswich, Queensland 4305, Australia (E-mail: noel.scott@uq. edu.au). Eric Laws is Adjunct Professor, Department of Tourism, James Cook University, Cairns, Queensland, Australia (E-mail: e.laws@runbox.com).

[Haworth co-indexing entry note]: "Understanding and Sharing Knowledge of New Tourism Markets: The Example of Australia's Inbound Chinese Tourism." Pan, Grace W., Noel Scott, and Eric Laws. Co-published simultaneously in *Journal of Quality Assurance in Hospitality &·Tourism* (The Haworth Hospitality Press, an imprint of The Haworth Press, Inc.) Vol. 7, No. 1/2, 2006, pp. 99-116; and: *Knowledge Sharing and Quality Assurance in Hospitality and Tourism* (ed: Noel Scott and Eric Laws) The Haworth Hospitality Press, an imprint of The Haworth Press, Inc., 2006, pp. 99-116. Single or multiple copies of this article are available for a fee from The Haworth Document Delivery Service [1-800-HAWORTH, 9:00 a.m. - 5:00 p.m. (EST). E-mail address: docdelivery@haworthpress.com].

Available online at http://jqaht.haworthpress.com
© 2006 by The Haworth Press, Inc. All rights reserved.
doi:10.1300/J162v07n01_06

KEYWORDS. China, Australia, knowledge, market intelligence, inbound tourism

INTRODUCTION

Tourism operators and State Tourism Offices (STOs) see the Chinese outbound tourist market as a great opportunity. The growth of China's economy is leading to a rapid growth in international travel from a burgeoning middle class. Many countries are seeking to tap into the China market. STOs from countries such as Australia, Canada, Fiji, and the UK, are all actively developing the potential of the Chinese market. This paper examines collection analysis and dissemination of market intelligence as components of knowledge management as a key step in the process.

Knowledge management is said to be the wave of the future. As tourism matures as an industry, it is vital that it adopts a 'knowledge-based' platform upon which to make its commercial and policy decisions (Cooper, 2005; Jafari, 1990). Knowledge management may be defined as:

> The coming together of organisational processes, information processing technologies, organisational strategies and culture for the enhanced management and leverage of human knowledge and learning for the benefit of the company. (Ahmed, Lim, & Loh, 2002:12)

The process of knowledge management has been conceptualized as a four stage process (Wiig, 1997). These are the top-down monitoring and facilitation of knowledge-related activities; creation and maintenance of the knowledge infrastructure; renewing, organizing, and transforming knowledge assets and leveraging (using) knowledge assets to realize their value. Within the process of knowledge management, the collection of information is a basic step on which other steps depend. Collection of market intelligence is also a basic function of a market oriented firm (Kennedy, Goolsby, & Arnould, 2003). This paper examines the general characteristics of market intelligence requirements applied to tourism, and the availability of this intelligence on the China outbound tourism market to Australia. It identifies gaps in the information available and discusses issues to be addressed to better target this market.

MARKET INTELLIGENCE

The literature of marketing and strategy stresses the importance of competitive market intelligence in shaping decisions (Dickson, 1992; Jaworski, Macinnis, & Kohli, 2002) and building market-oriented organizations (Day, 1990; Farrell & Oczkowski, 2002; Kennedy et al., 2003; Kirca, Jayachandran, & Bearden, 2005). Makadok and Barney (2001) discuss the importance of setting strategy based on accurate information.

Market intelligence is defined as information obtained from external sources that can be used for identifying problems, changes and opportunities in the external market environment (Talvinen & Saarinen, 1995; Wee, 2001). The terms 'business intelligence,' 'market intelligence' and 'competitor intelligence' are used interchangeably (Wood, 2001). Makadok and Barney (2001) discuss the importance of distinguishing between market intelligence acquisition and strategy formulation and note that an important contribution to strategy is an assessment of the extent of market information collection by a business.

WHAT INFORMATION DO WE NEED?

There are a number of typologies that may be used to guide the collection of market intelligence on China. For example, Low and Tan (1995) suggest that information needs may be described in terms of the external political, economic, social and cultural, competitive, demographic and technological environments as well as information about the marketing mix (facilities, personnel, power, public relations, promotions, place, price, product, process management and physical facilities). In an extensive study Ritchie and Ritchie (2002) discuss a number of types of information requirements for a region. They recommend undertaking a three step process consisting of an information needs assessment, an inventory of information sources and specification of key research tasks.

Further it is important to consider the level of analysis available for information. In business, information collected relates to a firm. Typically, in tourism information has been collected based on the destination country. Recently, devolution of responsibility for economic development has led to the idea that regions compete with one another suggesting that regions should be the focus for selecting information needed. Additionally, prior work by (Scott, 2002; 2003) suggests that it may be

DOUGLAS COLLEGE LIBRARY

better to collect and analyse information with reference to a particular destination or type of product because this helps understand how trends will affect particular groups of operators. This in turn emphasises the importance of formation of clusters of knowledge sharing businesses as a competitive strength.

MARKET INTELLIGENCE THROUGH SHARING?

The tourism sector has certain characteristics that both require constant flows of information about the customer and yet make knowledge sharing problematic. Firstly it is geographically dispersed with many small operators requiring customer information to be exchanged in order to facilitate travel and yet those involved may be ill-disposed to sharing of information (Department of Industry Tourism and Resources, 2003; Smith, 1991). A second related problem is generally poor market intelligence systems. Previous research has suggested that the market intelligence systems of tourism operators are rudimentary (Wood, 2001). The tourism sector is characterised by operators that are more operationally focused than market orientated. This results in decisions that are reliant on managers' prior knowledge and their contacts rather than 'hard' facts and data. However, this reinforces the importance of accurate information exchange making 'contacts' critical to business success.

A third problem is that there is a need to distinguish between the market intelligence needs of distribution channel members and destination operators. For example, it would appear that the trade channel members are in a better position to provide overseas market information than the tourism operator in a destination although Magnusson and Nilsson (2003) suggest sharing among trade channel members may be problematic. It appears that to some extent that knowledge in these groups is a source of power. Finally, even if available, examples of a poor use of information have been identified. Olsen and Zhao (2004) discuss the lack of use of strategic planning information in the hospitality sector. This is especially noted at the regional and local level where there maybe less extensive tourism managerial experience and skills. When the China outbound market was first open to Australia, the Australian government tourism agency did not take the immediate proactive approach of strategically planning the development of the market, instead, a rather "wait and see" approach was adopted.

THE DEVELOPMENT OF CHINESE OUTBOUND TOURISM

The Chinese Government placed tight restrictions on the outbound tourism market until 1983. Thereafter, following a pattern observed in many socialist economies, a slightly liberalised policy was adopted, first allowing Chinese leisure travel to Hong Kong and Macau, then in 1990 allowing visits to relatives and friends (VFR) in Thailand, Singapore and Malaysia (Dou & Dou, 1999). This VFR travel was extended to the Philippines in 1992. Next liberalization was applied by conferring Approved Destination Status (ADS) on Singapore, Malaysia and Thailand. Approved Destination Status means that China permits its residents to travel to selected countries for personal and leisure purposes usually on all-inclusive package tours. Subsequently, other Southeast Asian countries, such as the Philippines and South Korea, were also awarded ADS. In April 1999, Australia became the first western country opened up to the Chinese outbound tourism market followed soon afterwards by New Zealand. In 2004, a number of countries in Europe were granted ADS. There were 69 countries with ADS in July 2005 (Figure 1). As detailed in Appendix 1, ADS countries have spread to include Asia, Australasia, Europe, South America and Africa.

Most ADS countries are open to China nationwide, except for Australia and New Zealand which are open only to limited regions in China.

FIGURE 1. The Number of Countries Granted ADS by the Chinese Government

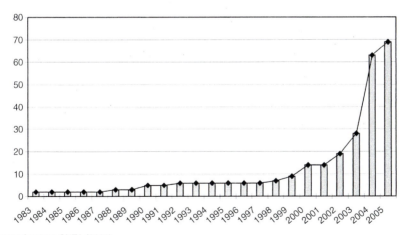

Source for data: CNTA (2005)

When Chinese citizens from Beijing, Shanghai and Guangdong Province[1] intend to travel overseas for leisure purposes, they must arrange the tour through authorised Chinese travel agents and travel in a group. The Chinese authorised travel agents apply for ADS visas on behalf of the tourists. If Chinese citizens travel to Australia for other purposes, such as business, education and VFR, they may arrange their tours through either authorised or unauthorised Chinese travel agents, but they have to obtain their visas on their own. Therefore, the mainstream business of the Chinese inbound travel trade to Australia is the ADS group market, whereas inbound travel for non-ADS purposes is a relatively small niche market. The number of Chinese outbound tourists in organised tour groups was over 3.5 million in 2001, or 30.45 percent of the total Chinese outbound tourists (CNTA, 2002).

A typical all-inclusive package includes international travel, private chartered coach within Australia, sightseeing excursions, local guides, accommodation and meals (mainly Chinese food with some Australian style meals). This form of tour arrangement can be compared with typical Western inclusive holiday packages (Laws, 1997) providing Chinese clients with similar advantages, particularly the benefit of knowing beforehand what to budget for their holiday, and relieving them of the anxiety of making their own arrangements in a foreign country. The introduction of so-called "Golden Weeks"; three standardised one-week long holidays has also boosted the development of the Chinese outbound tourism market (Zhang, 1997). These are International Labour Day (1 May- 7 May), National Day (1 Oct-7 Oct) and Chinese New Year (also called Spring Festival). As a result of these developments, the total number of Chinese outbound tourists has grown rapidly (Figure 2). The World Tourism Organisation has forecast that China will have 100 million outbound travellers and become the fourth largest source of outbound travel in the world by 2020 (World Tourism Organisation, 2003).

Mainland China has been acknowledged as an important emerging market by the Australian inbound tourism industry. The number of Chinese arrivals in Australia has increased at an average rate of 25.9 percent each year since 1985, reaching 251,300 in 2004 (Australian Bureau of Statistics (ABS), 2005) (Figure 3). Over 160,000 Chinese ADS visitors in approximately 10,500 groups have travelled to Australia since 1999 (Department of Industry, Tourism and Resources (DITR), 2005). While Chinese visitors accounted for only one percent of all international tourists visiting Australia in 1995 (Bureau of Tourism Research (BTR), 1996) it is expected to grow at 16% per annum for the next de-

FIGURE 2. Total Chinese Outbound Tourists 1994-2003

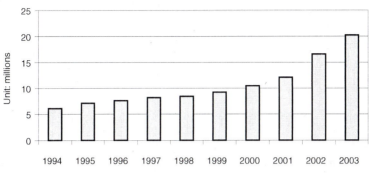

Source for data: National Bureau of Statistics (2004)

FIGURE 3. Short-Term Movement–Arrivals of Chinese Visitors to Australia 1985-2004 Base: All Visitors

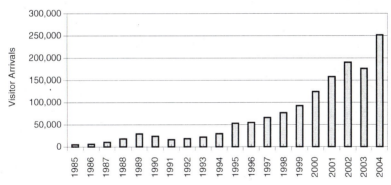

Source for data: ABS (1989; 2005)

cade, reaching approximately 1.2 million Chinese visitors per year by 2014 (Tourism Forecasting Committee, 2005). Moreover, Chinese visitors are now amongst the highest spending international visitors to Australia, spending an average of A$5,800 in 2003 (Tourism Research Australia, 2003). It is forecast that the economic value from Chinese tourists will reach $5.9 billion annually by 2014 (Tourism Forecasting Committee, 2005).

RESEARCH INTO CHINESE OUTBOUND TOURISM

An increasing number of studies have been conducted into the Chinese outbound tourism market. Early studies focused on obstacles to outbound travel from China as obtaining an exit visa was a major obstacle to expanding the outbound travel market from China at that time (Karwacki, Deng, and Chapdelaine, 1997; Zhou, King and Turner, 1997; Wang and Sheldon, 1995). Liberalisation of policy restrictions such as the relaxation of foreign currency exchange restriction and easier passport regulations were found to be required to encourage Chinese tourists visiting other countries (Karwacki et al., 1997; Zhou et al., 1997). Other researchers such as Wang and Sheldon (1995) performed more general studies into the determinants, trends and characteristics of Chinese outbound travel. Guo and Turner (2001) examined the structure of the Chinese outbound travel industry, and occasioned from China's entry into the World Trade Organisation.

Some academic studies on the Mainland Chinese tourists to Hong Kong were conducted during this early period of increasing travel. For example, Qu and Lam (1997) used the 12 years (1984-1995) annual time series data of "number of Mainland Chinese tourist arrivals," "China disposable income per capita," "consumer price indices in Hong Kong and China" and "exchange rate" to develop a travel demand model for Mainland Chinese tourists to Hong Kong. Zhang and Lam (1999) investigate Mainland Chinese visitors' motivations to visit Hong Kong by using push and pull factors. The study identifies a significant relationship between travel motivations and social demographic factors.

As Australian authorities became aware of the potential for inbound Chinese tourism, research was conducted on which to develop strategies. For example, the Australian Governments' Bureau of Tourism Research examined China's economy and its tourism market to Australia (Chai, 1996). This research sought to identify the economic characteristics of Chinese outbound tourism including the affordability of trips to Australia and hence estimated the size of the potential market. After the introduction of ADS to Australia, Pan and Laws (2001a; 2001b) conducted a study to identify the characteristics of Chinese travel patterns and of Chinese tourists in the Chinese ADS tourism market to Australia.

Similar studies although somewhat later were conducted in New Zealand. Ryan and Mo (2001) conducted a study to investigate the demographic profiles and motives of Chinese visitors to New Zealand. The study surveyed 400 visitors from mainland China, and identified that those who visited New Zealand are in a well-travelled segment, have above-average levels of income, are interested in seeing and visiting new places and may explore educational and business opportunities while on the trip.

As the Chinese market developed, Pan and Laws (2003) examined ways to develop Australia as a preferred destination for Chinese tourists vis-à-vis other destinations. They concluded that niche markets may be developed such as Meetings Incentives, Conventions and Exhibitions (MICE) to attract higher spending segments. Although the ADS mass tourism market from China has always been the focus of the Australian stakeholders, developing niche markets could diversify tourist products that Australia could offer to the China market to supplement the marginal profits from China ADS mass travel to Australia.

In addition, Pan and Laws (2001a; 2001b; 2003) also note that one of the critical issues for Australian inbound tour operators expanding their market share in the Chinese outbound tourism market is to establish and maintain appropriate business relationships with their Chinese counterparts. The findings from Pan (2004)'s study challenge previous literature on the role of guanxi (literally translated as personal relationships), which has been traditionally considered the most important thing in doing business with China, might not be as important as is claimed in most of the guanxi literature (for instance, Kotler, 1998; Lovett, Simmons, and Kali, 1999) in the Chinese outbound market to Australia. The findings reveal that Chinese travel agents have mixed responses with respect to the involvement of personal relationships in the meaning of guanxi, and the importance of guanxi in the process of developing partnership relationships with their Australian counterparts.

Zhang (2005) conducted a study to identify the characteristics of Chinese tourists' choice of a destination and the ways to draw more potential tourists to the less frequented destination. The study examined the marketing effectiveness of the Goldfields in Victoria, Australia and Tourism Victoria toward the Chinese market as a case study. Different characteristics of Chinese tourists by gender and age groups were identified; consequently different marketing techniques need to be applied to attract Chinese tourists to those rural destinations.

With an increase in the competitive ADS destinations noted earlier, Australia is facing challenges to maintain its market share in the China market. One of the key issues, which both academics (Pan & Laws, 2001a; Pan, 2004) and the industry (Tourism Australia) have drawn attention to, is quality issues reflecting on the satisfaction level and profitability of the market. In June 2005, the Chinese and Australian

Governments agreed on the amendments to the ADS scheme in order to sustain the quality of products and services provided to Chinese tourists and protect future growth (DITR, 2005). Under this regime, ADS code of business standards has been established. The China ADS Joint Monitoring Group, including representatives from the Department of Immigration and Multicultural and Indigenous Affairs, Department of Industry, Tourism & Resources, Tourism Australia and Australian Tourism Export Council nominated representatives of the states and territories; and nominated industry representatives, has been developed to provide fair competitions between operators and shops, and to provide knowledge and choices to Chinese inbound tourists.

INFORMATION AVAILABLE

This discussion indicates that there is a collection of data available on the Chinese market that has moved focus with the developments in outbound tourism. In order to examine if the factors discussed in the literature were also available to the industry, three tourism authority websites were examined and results shown in Table 2. These three websites were chosen as one is the national tourism peak body website (Tourism Research Australia–TRA), and two regional tourism peak body websites with the biggest number of Chinese leisure tourists (Tourism Queensland–QLD and Tourism New South Wales–NSW). The information on these websites was analysed using the categories provided by Low and Tan (2005). The results indicate information was primarily available at the national level for all websites with some items that Low and Tan (2005) consider important missing from the table. Further, no information from the academic literature shown in Table 1 was present or referred to on the websites.

The results of this brief analysis indicate that academic research topics have changed over time and focused on the characteristics of Chinese tourists travel patterns, the quality services provided by tour guides, product and destination development, and issues related to business-to-business relationships between Chinese and Australian travel operatives. These appear to be issues of interest to tourism operators. However, a lack of knowledge sharing between academic researchers and industry tourism offices is noted based on information and issues available on tourism websites. Further these websites do not contain all information considered useful according to Low and Tan (2005).

TABLE 1. Outline of Literature on the Chinese Inbound Travel Market to Australia

Authors	Topics	Method	Policy implications
Chai 1996	Economic characteristics of Chinese visitors (prior to ADS)	Analysing secondary data	Possibility of tapping into the China market
Guo and Turner 2001	Structure of Chinese outbound travel industry	N/A	Implications for foreign investors entering into the Chinese travel market
Ryan and Mo 2001	Motivations (for NZ visits)	Survey with Chinese visitors in New Zealand	Understanding the Chinese tourists decision-making process
Yu, Weiler and Ham 2001; 2004	Role of Australian tour guides Cultural mediation in guided tour experiences	Mix method (semi-structure interviews and survey) with tour guides and Chinese visitors in Australia	Training tour guides
Pan and Laws 2001a; 2001b; 2003	Chinese travel demand to Australia Destination marketing	Semi-structured interviews with Australian inbound tour operators	Unique travel patterns for Chinese tourists Tourist product development "Australian brand" development Quality issues Developing niche markets Developing appropriate business relationships
Pan 2004; Pan and Sparks 2004	Business relationships with Chinese travel agents and Australian inbound tour operators	Semi-structured interviews with Chinese travel agents and Australian inbound tour operators	Understanding the process of developing relationships cross-culturally Business ethics
March 2004	Business ethics in the Chinese inbound travel to Australia	Semi-structured interviews with industry participants in China and Australia	Unethical practices in the Chinese outbound business
Zhang 2005	International destination choice and its application to a less frequented destination model	Survey in rural attraction places, e.g. Goldfields region in Victoria, Australia	Marketing Chinese tourists to the less frequented destination in Australia

Three practical observations can be made on the basis of the present review. Firstly, there is a need for future research on emerging tourist markets to adopt a more systemic approach to the various issues identified in this growing area of literature. In particular, the China markets need to be examined to identify attractive segments. Very little tourism segmentation work has been done and this appears important for effective marketing. Secondly, the outcomes of research on the China market to Australia could have implications for other ADS destinations, and it might be useful for apparent competitors to pool their understanding of

TABLE 2. Issues Discussed on Tourism Authority Websites in Australia

	Description	Example	TA f	QLD f	NSW f
			Level g	Level g	Level g
Environment					
Political	The nature of the governance for the nation and the tourism sector.	Leadership; ADS	1		
Economic	The status of the GDP	GDP growth	1, a		
Social and cultural	The social and cultural developments	History & contemporary development		1	
Competitive	Competition for holidays within China from other categories of purchase and from other holiday destinations	Competition between Australian and other ADS destinations	1		
Demographic	Trends in age, etc over the next 10 years				
Technological	Impact of technology	Internet travel	1		
Marketing mix					
Facilities	Offices and budgets	Offices in China b	1	1	1
Personnel	Australian representatives and sales calls	Tel & Fax	1	1	1
Power	Perceived importance of Australian representatives				
Public relations	Knowledge and attitude to holiday in Australia's destinations	Media exposure of Australia	2		2
Promotions	Effect of various promotional activities d	Marketing activities	2	1	
Place.	Travel agents and distribution channels	Marketing partners	2		2
Price	Price sensitivity	Price change. Cost-conscious	1	1	
Product	Type of products suitable for various consumer segments— segmentation	Self-Drive, Incentive tour, study tour	1		1
Process management	Information systems, booking systems etc.				
Physical facilities	airports, airlines	Airline issues, air capacity	2		
Visitor profile		Demographic statistics; arrivals, expenditure	AUS 2; CHN 1, e	AUS 2; CHN 1	1

a: Mentioned different disposable income between regions
b: Including offices in Hong Kong, which are in charge of the business in China
c: Victoria Trade & Investment Office
d: No effect was mentioned, only activities.
e: Breakdown of statistics was available in terms of AUS states; no breakdown in terms of different Chinese tourist generating regions.
f: TA = Tourism Australia, QLD = Tourism Queensland, NSW = Tourism New South Wales
g: 1: national level 2: regional level.
Categories for Table adopted from Low and Tan (1995).

this complex market because in the longer term it is likely that Chinese outbound tourism will become the dominant market place for most destination countries. However, apart from the practical difficulty of getting competitors to collaborate, there is also the more fundamental theoretical problem of to what degree, if any, the problems and solutions applicable in any one ADS destination might apply to the others? Finally, while some research on China is available it does not appear to meet all user needs. Information relevant to local and regional tourism managers in Australia is not readily available. This is related to the issue of the type of information available. Most data is collected for Australia as a whole and data about interest in particular regions and their products are not available. As an example detailed information about the potential market for a particular aviation sector between a port in China and a port in Australia is not available.

CONCLUSION AND FURTHER RESEARCH

Knowledge availability does not necessarily lead to knowledge use (van Birgelen, de Ruyter, & Wetzels, 2001). In the case of the Chinese tourist market to Australia, findings from academic research and industry research by the National Tourist Office, (Tourism Australia) have helped to develop relevant policy to regulate the China market to Australia. For example, as discussed previously, the recent revised Agreement on the ADS Arrangement to Australia was based on extensive academic and industry research findings to tighten the quality control and enhance Chinese tourists' experiences in Australia.

The discussion has highlighted that while significant useful knowledge is available, there are issues in its dissemination to the industry. Further, some information of interest to the industry in regional areas is not available. Currently there is no mechanism to identify and prioritize information on this important market. The identification of such information needs would mean that the information available for sharing would be much more useful. Further, there is no template or list of information that could be usefully collected to boost information usefulness available. While some attempts to classify tourism knowledge have been made (Scott, 1999), there is no general use of such categorization schemes to allow knowledge requirements to be identified. Development of such a scheme would be of great practical and theoretical value to tourism.

Further, the evidence presented in this paper suggests that Australia's knowledge infrastructure with regard to its inbound Chinese markets can be improved. There is activity in the fundamental stage of collection of information and creation of knowledge, with the university sector taking steps to initiate research and disseminate their findings, largely to other academics. On the other hand it is not evident that the tourism knowledge thus generated is being effectively transformed into industry action, nor does it seem to leverage, that is to say, enhance the commercial success of operators or destinations. In terms of Wiig's (1997) knowledge management model, there is limited dialogue between researchers and the tourist organizations which could benefit from detailed knowledge of the Chinese inbound market. This has the twin results that some research has no apparent linkage to industry needs, while the research needs of industry members are not well reflected in the projects documented here, nor in those which are currently underway. In other words, the often-cited gap between academic research and industry re-occurs in this specific market, both with respect to what studies are carried out, and in how the findings of research are utilised at the industry level. The problem of geographic dispersion of operators and the suggested solution of clustering may have a special significance for Chinese–serving operators. There is an opportunity for innovative techniques to disseminate information specific to this sector, perhaps through an industry news-sheet or an expert seminar which tours the main destination areas.

Secondly, it was suggested that many operators are more operationally focused than market orientated. This can be seen in the failure to present their services in ways which appeal to Chinese groups, instead relying on traditional, general product concepts. It may be that this resistance to market sensitivity can only be overcome when its consequences become apparent through the drift, or migration, of Chinese tourists to alternative destinations and products.

The third issue, distinguishing the market intelligence needs of distribution channel members and destination operators is evident in the lack of understanding and trust between Chinese outbound operators and their Australian network partners. In the face of rapidly increasing competition from alternative destinations, better ways have to be found to educate both the Chinese and the Australian partners about each others business practices, expectations and needs.

The fourth issue, lack of extensive tourism managerial experience and skills, is a general concern of State and Commonwealth tourism administrators. What the recent development of the China inbound sector has done is to expose resistance to new ways of operating, lack of interest in findings from research could be of assistance in day-to-day operations, and the lack of a strategic approach to tourism management which characterizes many, but by no means all operators. Taken together these indicate practical and theoretical areas for further research and development to capitalize on the Chinese market.

NOTE

1. The ADS group tourism program was expanded to nine regions in China in November, 2003. The six new Chinese regions are Chongqing, Tianjin, Hebei Province, Zhe Jiang Province, Jiangsu Province and Shandong Province (Australian Tourist Commission, 2003).

REFERENCES

Ahmed, P. Lim, K., & Loh, A.. (2002). Learning Through Knowledge Management. Oxford: Butterworth Heinemann.

Australian Tourist Commission (2003). Australian Tourism Industry Conducts Mission to North Asia. ATC Online–Tourism Industry Essentials. 13 November 2003. Available at http://atc.australia.com/newcenter.asp?art = 4785

Bureau of Tourism Research (1996). China's Economy and Tourism to Australia. BTR conference paper 96.9.

Chai, P. (1996). China's Economy and Tourism to Australia. Bureau of Tourism Research conference paper.

China National Tourism Administration (2002, 2005). China Tourism Annual Report. Beijing, National Tourism Administration of the People's Republic of China (in Chinese).

China National Tourism Administration (2003). List of ADS Countries. Available at http://www.cnta.gov.cn/chujing/chujing.htm (in Chinese).

Cooper, C. (2005). Managing Tourism Knowledge: Concepts and Approaches. London: Channelview.

Cornish, S. (1997). Strategies for the acquisition of market intelligence and implications for the transferability of information inputs. Annals of the Association of American Geographers, 87(3), 451-470.

Davies, H., T. Leung, S. Luke and Y. Wong (1995). The Benefits of "Guanxi": The Value of Relationships in Developing the Chinese Market. Industrial Marketing Management, 24: 207-214.

Day, G. S. (1990). Market Driven Strategy. New York: Free Press.

Department of Industry Tourism and Resources. (2003). A Medium to Long Term Strategy for Tourism. Canberra: Department of Industry, Tourism and Resources.

Dickson, P. R. (1992). Toward a General Theory of Competitive Rationality. Journal of Marketing, 56(January), 69-83.

Department of Industry Tourism and Resources. (2005). China Approved Destination Status (ADS) Scheme. Canberra: Australian Government.

Dou, Q. and J. Dou (1999). A Study of the Chinese Mainland Outbound Tourist Markets. Asia Pacific Tourism Association Fifth Annual Conference, Hong Kong.

Dunfee, T. W. and D. E. Warren (2001). Is Guanxi Ethical? A Normative Analysis of Doing Business in China. Journal of Business Ethics, 32: 191-204.

Farrell, M., & Oczkowski, E. (2002). Are Market Orientation and Learning Orientation Necessary for Superior Organizational Performance? Journal of Market-Focused Management, 5(3), 197– 217.

Guo, W. and L. W. Turner (2001). Entry strategies into China for foreign travel companies. Journal of Vacation Marketing, 8(1): 49-63.

Hofstede, G. (1980). Culture's Consequences: International Differences in Work-Related Values. Newbury Park, CA: Sage.

Hofstede, G. (1991). Cultures and Organizations: Software of the Mind. Berkshire, UK: McGraw-Hill.

Jafari, J. (1990). Research and scholarship: The basis of tourism education. Journal of Tourism Studies, 1(1), 33-41.

Jaworski, B. J., Macinnis, D. J., & Kohli, A. K. (2002). Generating Competitive Intelligence in Organizations. Journal of Market-Focused Management, 5(4), 279-307.

Karwacki, J., Deng, S., & Chapdelaine C. (1997) The tourism markets of the four dragons–a canadian perspective. Tourism Management, 18(6): 373-383.

Kennedy, K. N., Goolsby, J. R., & Arnould, E. J. (2003). Implementing a Customer Orientation: Extension of Theory and Application. Journal of Marketing, 67(4), 67-81.

Kirca, A. H., Jayachandran, S., & Bearden, W. O. (2005). Market Orientation: A Meta-Analytic Review and Assessment of Its Antecedents and Impact on Performance. Journal of Marketing, 69(2), 24-41.

Kotler, P. (1998). Marketing. 4th edition. New York and Sydney: Prentice Hall.

Laws, E. (1997). Managing Packaged Tourism. UK and USA: International Thomson Business Press.

Lovett, S., L. C. Simmons and R. Kali (1999). Guanxi Versus the Market: Ethics and Efficiency (Chinese system of doing business based on personal relationships). Journal of International Business Studies, 30(2): 231-242.

Low, S. P., & Tan, M. C. S. (1995). A convergence of Western marketing mix concepts and oriental strategic thinking. Marketing Intelligence & Planning, 13(2), 36-46.

Magnusson, J., and Nilsson, A. (2003). To Facilitate or Intervene–A Study of Knowledge Management Practice in SME Networks. Journal of Knowledge Management Practice, 4. (http:www.tlainc.com/jkmp4.htm accessed 25/7/2005).

Makadok, R., & Barney, J. B. (2001). Strategic Factor Market Intelligence: An Application of Information Economics to Strategy Formulation and Competitor Intelligence. Management Science, 47(12), 1621-1638.

March, R. (2004). Modelling Unethical Marketing Practices in the Outbound Chinese Travel Market. Conference Proceedings of Tourism State of the Art II, 27-30 June 2004, The Scottish Hotel School, University of Strathclyde.

National Bureau of Statistics (2004). 2004 Chinese Statistics Yearbook. Beijing: China Statistics Press.

Olsen, M. D., & Zhao, J. (2004). Industry Change, Environmental Scanning and Firm Strategy: How is the Hospitality Industry Doing? Tourism and Hospitality Planning & Development, 1(1), 13-18.

Pan, G.W. (2004) Business Partnership Relationships in the Chinese Inbound Tourism Market to Australia, PhD thesis, Griffith University, Gold Coast, Australia.

Pan, G. ,W. and E. Laws (2001a). Tourism Marketing Opportunities for Australia in China. Journal of Vacation Marketing, 8(1): 39-48.

Pan, G. W. and E. Laws (2001b). Attracting Chinese Outbound Tourists: Guanxi and the Australian Preferred Destination Perspective. In Tourism Distribution Channels: Practices, Issues and Transformations. Edited by Buhalis, D. and E. Laws. London and New York: Continuum, 282-297.

Pan, G.W. and Laws, E. (2003). Tourism Development of Australia as a Sustained Preferred Destination for Chinese Tourists, Asia Pacific Journal of Tourism Research, 8(1):37-47.

Pan, G.W. and Sparks, B. (2003). Cross-Cultural Differences–Does It Matter in The Sino-Australian Tourism Distribution Channel? Proceedings of the 9th Asia Pacific Tourism Association Annual Conference. Sydney, Australia, 780-786.

Parker, D. (2000). Can Government CI Bolster Regional Competitiveness? Competitive Intelligence Review, 11(4), 57-64.

Park, S. H. and Y. Luo (2001). Guanxi and Organizational Dynamics: Organizational Networking in Chinese Firms. Strategic Management Journal, 22: 455-477.

Qu, H. and S. Lam (1997). A Travel Demand Model for Mainland Chinese Tourists to Hong Kong. Tourism Management, 18(8): 593-597.

Redding, S. G. (1993). The Spirit of Chinese Capitalism. Berlin and New York: Walter de Gruyter.

Ritchie, R., & Ritchie, J. R. B. (2002). A framework for an industry supported destination marketing information system. Tourism Management, 23, 439-454.

Ryan, C. and X. Mo (2001). Chinese visitors to New Zealand–Demographics and perceptions. Journal of Vacation Marketing, 8(1): 13-27.

Scott, N. (1999). Tourism Research in Australia. Gold Coast: Cooperative Research Centre for Sustainable Tourism.

Scott, N. (2002). Product market perspective of self-drive tourism. In D. Carson, I. Waller & N. Scott (Eds.), Drive Tourism: up the wall and round the bend (pp. 81-90). Altona, Victoria: Common Ground Publishing Pty Ltd.

Scott, N. (2003, 5-8th February). Trends in tourism: Evolution of tourism product markets. Paper presented at the CAUTHE Conference, Coffs Harbour.

Simmons, L. C. and J. M. Munch (1996). Is Relationship Marketing Culturally Bound: A Look at Guanxi in China. Advances in Consumer Research, 23: 92-96.

Smith, S. L. J. (1991). The supply-side definition of tourism: Reply to Leiper. Annals of Tourism Research, 18, 312-314.

Svensson, G. and G. Wood (2003). The Dynamics of Business Ethics: A Function of Time and Culture–Cases and Models. Management Decisions, 41(4): 350-361.

Tallman, S., Jenkins, M., Henry, N., & Pinch, S. (2004). Knowledge, clusters and competitive advantage. Academy of Management Review, 29(2), 258-271.

Talvinen, J., & Saarinen, T. (1995). MkIS support for the marketing management process: Perceived improvements for marketing management. Market Intelligence and Planning, 13(1), 18-17.

Tourism Australia (2005). China Monthly Market Report. May 2005, Eastern Hemisphere, Tourism Australia.

Tourism Forecasting Committee. (2005). Inbound Tourism Forecasts–2005 to 2014. Canberra: Tourism Research Australia.

Tourism Research Australia. (2003). International visitor survey. Canberra.

van Birgelen, M., de Ruyter, K., & Wetzels, M. (2001). What Makes Service Research Centers Effective? Journal of Service Research, 3(3), 265-273.

Wang, Y. and P. Sheldon (1995). The Sleeping Dragon Awakes: The Outbound Chinese Travel Market. Journal of Travel & Tourism Marketing, 4(4): 41-54.

Wee, T. (2001). The use of marketing research and intelligence in strategic planning: Key issues and future trends. Marketing Intelligence & Planning, 19(4), 245-253.

Wiig, K. M. (1997). Knowledge Management: An Introduction and Perspective. The Journal of Knowledge Management, 1(1), 6-14.

Wood, E. (2001). Marketing information systems in tourism and hospitality small- and medium-sized enterprises: a study of Internet use for market intelligence. International Journal of Tourism Research, 3(4), 283-299.

World Tourism Organisation (2003). Chinese Outbound Tourism. Madrid.

Yu, X., B. Weiler and S. Ham (2001). Intercultural communication and mediation: A framework for analysing the intercultural competence of Chinese tour guides. Journal of Vacation Marketing, 8(1): 75-87.

Yu, X., B. Weiler and S. Ham (2004). Cultural Mediation in Guided Tour Experiences: A Case Study of Australian Guides of Chinese Tour Groups. Department of Management Working Paper Series. Monash University: 12 pages.

Zhang, W. (1997). China's Domestic Tourism: Impetus, Development and Trends. Tourism Management 18(8), 565-571.

Zhang, Y. (2005). Modelling International Tourists Destination Choice and Its Application to A Less Frequented Destination. Melbourne, Australia, La Trobe University.

Zhang, Q. H. and T. Lam (1999). An Analysis of Mainland Chinese Visitors' Motivations to Visit Hong Kong. Tourism Management, 20: 587-594.

Zhou, L., B. King and L. Turner (1997). The China Outbound Market: An Evaluation of Key Constraints and Opportunities. Journal of Vacation Marketing, 4(2): 109-119.

doi:10.1300/J162v07n01_06

Managing Knowledge in Tourism Planning: And How to Assess Your Capability

Stephen Clark

Noel Scott

SUMMARY. This paper explores the theme of strategic planning in a State Tourism Organization (STO) from a knowledge management perspective. It highlights the value of knowledge in strategy making and the importance of an organisation's knowledge management agenda in facilitating a strategic planning process. In particular, it considers the capability of an STO to implement knowledge management as the key to a successful strategic planning exercise. In order to develop greater insight into the factors that impact on planning competence, the key aim of this paper is to develop a framework on which the capability of a STO to implement a knowledge-based agenda in strategic planning can be assessed. Research on knowledge management in the field of tourism is limited and there is little practical account of the application of knowledge management principles in tourism planning. Further, there is no apparent tool or instrument that allows for the assessment of an STO's capability to implement knowledge management in planning initiatives.

Stephen Clark is Strategic Planning Manager, Tourism Queensland (E-mail: s2dc@tpg.com.au) and Noel Scott is Lecturer, The School of Tourism and Leisure Management, The University of Queensland, 11 Salisbury Road, Ipswich, 4305 Queensland, Australia (E-mail: noel.scott@uq.edu.au).

[Haworth co-indexing entry note]: "Managing Knowledge in Tourism Planning: And How to Assess Your Capability." Clark, Stephen, and Noel Scott. Co-published simultaneously in *Journal of Quality Assurance in Hospitality & Tourism* (The Haworth Hospitality Press, an imprint of The Haworth Press, Inc.) Vol. 7, No. 1/2, 2006, pp. 117-136; and: *Knowledge Sharing and Quality Assurance in Hospitality and Tourism* (ed: Noel Scott and Eric Laws) The Haworth Hospitality Press, an imprint of The Haworth Press, Inc., 2006, pp. 117-136. Single or multiple copies of this article are available for a fee from The Haworth Document Delivery Service [1-800-HAWORTH, 9:00 a.m. - 5:00 p.m. (EST). E-mail address: docdelivery@haworthpress.com].

Available online at http://jqaht.haworthpress.com
© 2006 by The Haworth Press, Inc. All rights reserved.
doi:10.1300/J162v07n01_07

Based on a literature review, a three-point framework of assessment is developed. The three elements of the framework are identified as:

1. Integration of knowledge management objectives with strategic imperatives;
2. A planning approach that balances top-down (outcome focused) with bottom-up (process focused) planning processes; and
3. Organisational capacity, including leadership, people and culture, process, technology, content and continuous improvement.

The framework is tested through application to a practical case study–a planning initiative undertaken by a leading tourism STO in Australia. The results demonstrate that the framework is a useful means to evaluate organisational capability in knowledge-led strategic planning exercises and would be of practical value as a point of reference for future knowledge- based strategic planning projects. doi:10.1300/J162v07n01_07 *[Article copies available for a fee from The Haworth Document Delivery Service: 1-800-HAWORTH. E-mail address: <docdelivery@haworthpress.com> Website: <http://www.HaworthPress.com> © 2006 by The Haworth Press, Inc. All rights reserved.]*

KEYWORDS. China, Australia, knowledge, market intelligence, inbound tourism

INTRODUCTION

Strategy making is a complex process (Mintzberg 1994). In moving from traditional normative models to a thinking approach to strategic planning, planners, according to Mintzberg (1994), need to embrace the learning that produces new perspectives and new ideas. Drew (1999) suggests that learning, strategic thinking and strategy can be enriched through knowledge. Strategy development, he maintains, can be enhanced through building a knowledge dimension into the various schools and tools of strategy. This move, he believes, is an important first step in developing and implementing a knowledge-based strategy that will create new knowledge driven sources of competitive advantage that deliver superior value to customers. Therefore knowledge management is fundamentally dependent on knowledge sharing.

This paper explores the theme of strategic planning in a State Tourism Organization (STO) from a knowledge management perspective (Quintas et al 1997; Drew 1999; Hall and Andriani 2002; Kakabadse et al 2001). In particular the paper examines an STO's capability to implement knowledge management as the key to a successful strategic planning exercise. Strategic planning and knowledge management are time intensive exercises that require proper planning and implementation. The aim of the paper is to provide organisations considering using knowledge management with advice on how to ensure they get a return on their investment.

Knowledge Management (KM) is a relatively new area of inter-disciplinary enquiry, emerging over the last decade with the evolution of the information economy and rapid advancements in technology. At the same time, ideas on strategy and strategic management have evolved to the point where there is a natural intersection between these fields of enquiry. Tourism has a developing KM research strand (Cooper 2005) but no practical account of the application of KM principles in a tourism planning context appears to have been published. Further, while the topic of the capacity of organisations to implement a knowledge agenda is discussed in the literature, there is no apparent tool or instrument that allows for the assessment of an organisation's capability to implement knowledge management in its strategic planning. In this paper, a three-point framework for analysis is developed and applied to a practical case study–involving a leading tourism agency's planning initiative.

STRATEGIC PLANNING AND KNOWLEDGE MANAGEMENT

If knowledge can enrich strategy and assist organisations to compete more effectively then how an organisation manages and mobilises its knowledge will have an impact on its success. Quintas et al (1997) believe that if knowledge is the focus, then organisations must find ways to manage the processes by which knowledge is created or acquired, communicated, applied and used. Managing knowledge, they say, is a process "of managing knowledge of all kinds to meet existing and emerging needs, to identify and exploit existing and acquired knowledge assets and to develop new opportunities" (p. 387).

Knowledge Management (KM), according to Awad and Ghaziri (2004) is the process of capturing and making use of the organisation's collective expertise anywhere in the business, whether it is on paper, in documents or in databases (explicit knowledge) or in people's heads (tacit knowledge). It is a process, they say, that integrates people, technology and organisational processes in the course of organising, refining and distributing knowledge throughout the organization.

The process for managing knowledge in an organisation has been described as a lifecycle process that consists of the following series of steps (Demarest 1997):

- Construction–the making of knowledge with complex processes
- Embodiment–the transformation of the knowledge that is tacit into processes and practices
- Dissemination: the distribution of embodied knowledge through an organisation or value chain
- Use–the application of disseminated, embodied knowledge to specific problems with an aim to produce results
- Management–the monitoring, measurement and intervention in the construction, embodiment, dissemination and use by knowledge managers.

Simply understanding the steps in the KM process or system is however, according to Knight and Howes (2003), not enough to generate benefit. The essence in any program to mobilise knowledge in an organisation, they believe, is to see how it can be applied to improve business performance. In this regard they view knowledge management strategy as being necessarily complementary to corporate strategy and the pursuit of corporate mission, goals and objectives. Awad and Ghaziri (2004) agree, believing that the nexus between business strategy and KM should be established early in the planning cycle so that it is incorporated into the framework of the company's strategic plan. In practical terms, this intersection between knowledge strategy and business strategy is described by Wiig (1997) as the application of the steps of the KM system in all plans, operations and activities to ensure that the best possible knowledge is available at each point of action.

The importance of a symbiotic relationship between knowledge as a strategic resource and organisational strategy is further reinforced by Standards Australia (2003). Achievement of this integration is, they suggest is dependent upon the capability and culture of an organisation and its capacity to implement a KM program. The relationship between culture and organisational effectiveness is well represented in the literature (Hofstede 1986; Barney 1986; Denison and Mishra 1995). In this regard Standards Australia (2003) highlight the value of establishing a culture that encourages knowledge-building skills and the development of strong, trusting knowledge creation and sharing networks as the elemental bridge between knowledge and organisational strategy. Grant (1997:452) reinforces this cultural perspective suggesting that an organisational environment that encourages the processes of knowledge creation, sharing and empowerment, is a necessary precondition for KM to flourish: "the principle management challenge is . . . . establishing the mechanisms by which cooperating individuals can coordinate their activities in order to integrate their knowledge into productive activity."

AN EVALUATION FRAMEWORK

As identified by Standards Australia (2003), the capacity of an organisation to implement KM is one of the crucial factors in leveraging the strategic value of knowledge and achieving a productive nexus between knowledge management and business strategy. Carson and Adams (2004) agree, suggesting that an organisation's ability to undertake specific knowledge management practices is directly related to its capacity to implement a KM agenda. Demarest (1997) elaborates; stating that an organisation's capacity to implement KM is dependent on durable internal infrastructure that includes robust cultural and technical systems that can assist the day-to-day processes of knowledge building.

A survey of the literature yields a number of key writers who discuss the issue of KM and organisational capacity, several of whom are summarised in Table 1.

Knight and Howes (2003:95), in an outline of their systematic framework for the management and delivery of knowledge management initiatives, identify similar capacity issues as illustrated in Table 1, describing them as "levers or enablers of KM change." Mobilising knowledge in an organisation, they say, requires getting the right ideas and technologies together to shape the new reality. Based on their ideas and the themes identified in Table 1, the capacity of organisations to implement KM programs can be summarised into the six key dimensions shown in Table 2.

Together, these factors form a practical framework by which organisations can assess their capacity to undertake knowledge management programs and develop the appropriate infrastructure to maximise the potential for successful implementation.

In summary, the literature review adds credence to the proposition that knowledge can have strategic value in business and further indicates that by establishing linkages between the principles of knowledge management and the process of strategic planning or strategy making, organisations may move toward achieving sustainable competitive ad-

TABLE 1. Themes in Organisational Capacity

	Quintas, Lefere & Jones (1997)	Demarest (1997)	Standards Australia (2003)	Carson & Adams (2004)
Technology	Concept maps, hypermedia and project oriented databases, artificial intelligence, approaches to knowledge acquisition, representation and discovery, the decision support, data mining and knowledge dissemination	information technology's primary strategic objective in a knowledge intensive organisation is to facilitate knowledge creation, embodiment, and dissemination, use and management and each of these five activities requires substantially different complexes of information technology to do its work	the use of technology as an enabler of KM	the uses of information and communication technology to manage knowledge pro-cesses
Organizational structure and people	The development of structures that facilitate the growth of communities of practice Training, development recruitment, motivation, retention, organization, job design, cultural change in the encouragement of thinking, participation and creativity	Knowledge management rewards embodiment and dissemination and incessant knowledge creation and so re-quires fundamental changes to deep-seated cultural givens in most organisations	Leadership Organisational design Values and belief systems	Setting the context and direction for the organizations KM initiatives The organizational culture and its influences on iterative learning and information sharing
Continuous improvement	Process innovation, reengineering; for both radical and continuous improvement	Knowledge management produces results only to the extent that the knowledge management infrastructure is installed, operational and capable of informing on itself	The means through which knowledge can be embedded in work processes to enhance organisational performance	The knowledge management implications of accreditation, reporting and other activities aimed at fostering continuous improvement
Other	**Leadership** setting the context and direc-tion for the organizations KM initiatives	**Operational infrastructure** Everything about a traditional human resources organization that much of conventional organizational design operations require retooling in a knowledge centered organisation	**Content** The appropriateness accessibility, accuracy, consistency, currency and quality of content the development and leveraging of intellectual capital Content applies to both explicit and tacit knowledge	**Infrastructure** The constraints of strategic knowledge management brought about by the infrastructure of policies processes and regulation

TABLE 2. Dimensions of Knowledge Management Programs

Dimension	
Leadership	Clear organisational leadership that • sets the context and direction for KM initiatives and provide a clear focus • promotes the values of the sharing and use of knowledge • fosters teamwork, trust and two way communication • manages organisational change
People & Culture	Structures and processes that support • communication and knowledge sharing skills; thinking and creativity • motivation and workplace attitude • learning and reward
Process	Organisational processes and systems that • improve knowledge identification, creation, use, sharing and recording • enhance the embedding of knowledge in work practices
Technology	Technological infrastructure that • enhances the gathering, storage and use of information • facilitates knowledge creation, embodiment, and dissemination and application • enhances communication, collaboration and decision making
Content	Availability of data and information that is • Relevant, accurate, current and of appropriate quality
Continuous Improvement	Capability of the organisational to • monitor performance and reflect on practice and experience • apply learning in practice as an ongoing process of improvement

vantage in complex, dynamic business environments. To maximise the opportunity however, the literature also suggests that an organisation's knowledge management agenda needs to be complementary to corporate strategy and its planning needs to be flexible enough to be able to accommodate both top-down and bottom up planning perspectives. It is proposed that an organisation's ability to implement a KM agenda rests on its capacity to do so, pointing to the six key factors or enablers shown in Table 2.

Applying the insights gained from the literature to the issue of implementation of knowledge management in strategic planning processes, a framework for evaluation emerges around three key ideas and is illustrated in Figure 1:

1. Integration of KM objectives with corporate strategic imperatives
2. A planning approach that balances top-down (outcome focused) with bottom up (process focused) planning processes
3. Organisational capacity involving leadership, people and culture, process, technology, content, continuous improvement

FIGURE 1. Framework for the Evaluation of Organisational Capability in Implementing a Knowledge Management Agenda

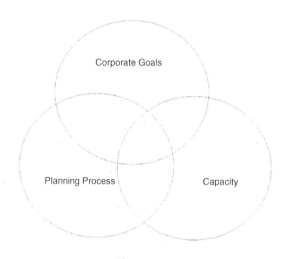

CASE STUDY

In order to test its validity, the paper applies this framework to a specific case example. Each element of the framework is discussed in light of this case. The discussion shows that the framework is a useful basis from which to analyse a strategic planning process from a knowledge management perspective.

The case selected to test this framework involved a destination management planning program being implemented by a State Tourism Office (STO) in Australia. This case was selected primarily on the basis that it is a practical example of a corporate planning exercise where the principles of knowledge management have been applied in a tourism strategic planning context. Due to the writers' direct involvement in the program, the main data collection method employed in this study is personal experience, observation and reflection. It is important to point out, however, that due to the team-based approach to planning and the processes of consultation and feedback with internal and external stakeholders, the data input is drawn from a range of experiences.

The STO is the State's peak tourism development and marketing body and was established in the 1970s as a statutory authority of the State Government under the jurisdiction of the Minister of Tourism. The organisation provides leadership and guidance to the State's tourism industry and delivers on the Government's tourism agenda through an integrated approach to tourism policy, destination development and marketing. The organisation's mission statement involves enhancing the development and marketing of the State's tourist destinations in partnership with industry, government and the community. Corporate business priorities are identified as: Destination Development and Marketing, Partnerships and Corporate Excellence.

The destination management planning program was an organisational response to a rapidly changing business environment. The program was conceived as a strategy to bring together the people and the experience, knowledge and skills in the organisation in a collaborative way to:

- achieve a more integrated, cross-functional approach to business planning
- produce a suite of integrated destination management plans designed provide leadership and direction to government and industry in order to facilitate sustainable tourism growth and industry profitability.

The initiative was an evolution of a marketing strategy instigated in the late 1990s. It represented a more integrated approach to understanding destination needs and the delivery of services. Early in the development of the concept, the principles of knowledge management were introduced to underpin the importance of the initiative as a strategic knowledge building exercise and to guide to the development of a comprehensive, collaborative planning process.

Plans for a number of destinations in the state have been prepared and published after a lengthy process of planning, consultation, feedback and review. The plans are described as researched based strategic documents intended to provide focus and direction for the development and marketing of the State's tourist destinations. They are designed to directly inform the business planning of departments and business units and are also intended to provide direction and sharing of knowledge for the business planning of partner and stakeholder organisations. In conjunction with the publication of the plans, a dynamic, web-based distribution system was developed, as the principle distribution mechanism.

USE OF THE EVALUATION FRAMEWORK

In this section, the case is analysed using the three key ideas outlined above. The discussion explores the planning initiative according to each of these key ideas, with particular attention given to the issue of organisational capacity. The primary purpose of this analysis is to determine whether the framework developed through the literature review has validity in practice and therefore has value in assessing other planning exercises and/or as a point of reference for planners when embarking on knowledge based strategic planning projects.

Integration of Knowledge Management Objectives with Corporate Strategic Imperatives

The outline of the planning initiative describes a strategic planning exercise consistent with the principles of Knowledge Management. In this regard, the intention of the program to engender a more inclusive, integrated approach to strategic planning and to produce a suite of plans designed to inform consistent decision making amongst stakeholders, appears to be fully aligned with the overarching mission of the Corporation and its strategic imperatives to enhance the marketing and development of the state's tourist destinations in partnership with stakeholders.

A Planning Approach that Balances Top-Down (Outcome Focused) with Bottom Up (Process Focused) Planning Processes

The planning program was an initiative of the Chief Executive Officer and Executive of the organisation. In the early stages of development a number of meetings were held amongst the Executive and the senior management team in order to discuss and develop the concept. A project manager was subsequently appointed to coordinate the initiative, develop the planning model and devise a planning process. Later, at a corporate management conference, the broader management group of the organisation was briefed on the intentions of the program and the expectations of the planning process.

While the model on which the final plan was to be based reflected standard, classical planning models outlined in general planning or management texts (e.g., Hill et al 2004), an inclusive planning process was designed to harness the skills and experience of staff from across the organisation and to gather important input from key external stakeholders.

In practice, five internal cross-functional planning teams were established, which worked for nine months to produce draft plans for each destination for which the STO was responsible. Following this, key external stakeholders in each destination were consulted and invited to provide feedback. Once received, the teams incorporated the feedback into each plan through an internal refresh and review process. The plans were then completed, signed-off by the Boards and management of each regional tourism organisation and subsequently published. At this stage, with the public release of the plans, measures are in place to extend stakeholder consultation in each destination as part of a review and revision process.

While the model on which each plan is based reflects a classical top-down approach to planning with a clear set of management expectations, the planning process reflects more of a processual or emergent planning approach. In this regard, as Hill et al (2004) suggest, the model moves towards achieving a balance between top-down and bottom-up planning approaches.

The planning process has not been without critics, with some criticism being leveled at the lack of wide industry and community consultation during the initial development stages of each plan. From an emergent planning perspective, the criticism has some validity. The merits or otherwise of the Agency's decision not to take the community based route to the development of the plans will likely be the source of debate for some time to come. Whether the planning approach stands up or not will likely rely on the rigour of the forthcoming stakeholder engagement program and the Agency's commitment to continuous improvement.

Overall, the planning model acknowledges the principle of a balanced top-down/bottom up approach although, depending on perspective, it could be viewed as not fully addressing this principle in practice. Given the valuable experience of the internal planning process and the external, albeit limited, consultation to date, this second factor is also considered a valid component of the assessment framework.

Organisational Capacity

Leadership

Organizational leadership that sets the context and direction for KM initiatives and provides a clear focus. The CEO and senior management group set the initial context and vision for the program. Early leadership initiatives included the appointment of a Project Manager and the appointment of five cross-functional planning teams and team leaders.

The early planning period proved quite challenging for the planning teams and after only two months it was apparent that the project was not going to meet its set deadlines. A meeting of the management group revealed that there was some resistance to implementation at senior and middle management level and a crisis of confidence at Executive level. Feedback from team members also indicated that department managers were giving mixed messages about the importance of the exercise and its business priority.

Despite early enthusiasm and the eventual emergence of a project champion, clarity focus and direction remained critical leadership issues throughout the program.

Organisational leadership that promotes the values of the sharing and use of knowledge. Against the background of a functional organisational structure and culture, the values of sharing and using knowledge were integral to the project planning philosophy. This was operationalised through a range of consultative mechanisms including the formation of cross-functional planning teams, a move designed to draw on expertise and experience from across the organisation in the development of each plan.

Despite intentions and supporting mechanisms, teams and team members found it difficult to overcome functional differences and to exchange experience, views and ideas in a creative, productive manner. Time and daily work pressures together with mixed messages from divisional and department management about the value of the team approach also inhibited the successful shift to cross-functional team based knowledge sharing and knowledge building.

The experience of this aspect of the program highlighted the importance of this aspect of the framework and the challenges of implementation.

Organisational leadership that fosters teamwork, trust and two-way communication. The encouragement of teamwork was an intrinsic aspect of the project however, as the project proceeded, it was apparent that teams struggled to work effectively and productively. While assistance with coordination and facilitation was provided, issues relating to the values of teamwork, the importance of team skills and the provision of sufficient resources to enable teams to work effectively remained a salient leadership concern.

With regard to communication, despite a range of mechanisms established to foster better communication within and between planning teams and between planning teams and project management, additional exercises to affirm direction, clarify issues and deal with problems and expectations were required.

Effective communication loomed as a critical issue throughout the process and on reflection it was considered that a more formal communication plan developed at the start of the program would have helped to ensure that the channels and tools for communication were clearly established and understood. As the project evolved, it also became apparent that a formal communication strategy would have helped to keep the whole of the organisation as well as key external stakeholders informed of progress.

Organisational leadership that manages organisational change. The project posed a number of challenges to the organisation, its structure, the roles and relationships of its staff and the manner in which it conducted its daily operations. In a review of progress of the initiative it transpired that many of the issues and challenges arising were similar to those experienced by organisations undergoing significant change (Stoner et al., 1985; Gibson et al., 2000). With this in mind, it was recommended that a change management strategy be implemented in parallel to the planning program in an effort to better deal with cultural difficulties and to promote a more favourable organisational climate. This recommendation was not adopted and cultural hygiene problems ensued.

Given the challenges posed by this project, effectively managing organisational change arises as a salient element of the evaluation framework.

People and Culture

Structures and processes that support communication and knowledge sharing skills; thinking and creativity. The establishment of cross-functional or process work teams, as suggested by Johannessen et al. (1997) was intended to engender better cross-departmental communication and knowledge sharing and to encourage better thinking and innovation in planning and practice. As discussed previously, the difficulty teams experienced in functioning effectively appeared to inhibit knowledge sharing and higher order activities of creative thinking and innovation. It was observed that the tactical, operational focus of the organisation and the pressures of day-to-day business inhibited the capacity of the organisation to support and promote knowledge sharing and the values of thinking and innovation.

Structures and processes that support motivation and workplace attitude. Despite the best efforts of a few committed individuals to promote the organisational values of the project, general motivation and attitude continued to be a vexing issue for most of the planning period. Given the challenging nature of the project and the pressures involved on top of day-to-day responsibilities, more regard could have been taken of the need to engender more a positive workplace motivation and attitude as integral aspects of a change management strategy.

Structures and processes that support learning and reward. Similar to the above issues, at the macro level the organisation has a range of programs that encourage individual learning and reward for achievement. At the team or work group level however recognition of the values of experiential learning in particular is not an overtly recognised part of organisational culture. Consequently the value of the project as an important learning exercise was not well regarded or acknowledged. Reward for effort at this level largely occurred on an ad hoc basis, as a reaction to circumstances rather than as an integral aspect of program management or organisational culture.

Process

Organisational processes and systems that improve knowledge identification, creation, use, sharing and recording. The key mechanism or process established to enhance the management of knowledge in this case was the establishment of five internal cross-functional planning teams, comprising of experienced practitioners drawn from various areas of the organisation. Teams were provided with a framework and methodology to guide their process and the recording of their work but were largely encouraged to be self-governing, within established protocols and timeframes. To monitor the progress of each team, a regular forum of team leaders was established–which also served as a learning exercise, informing on and enhancing the program and its implementation.

Once draft plans were completed a key stakeholder engagement and feedback process was undertaken. Feedback was recorded and processed by each team and incorporated into a review of each plan. Whilst most team members had first hand experience of the destinations on which they were working, the feedback from key external stakeholders was an essential aspect of the knowledge building, sharing and recording cycle. At this stage, with the completion of the initial round of plans, broader engagement of stakeholders is envisaged as part of a dynamic, iterative knowledge-building paradigm.

Organisational processes and systems that enhance the embedding of knowledge in work practices. An important consideration of the planning model was to ensure that the outcomes of and the insights gained from the planning process were applied directly in practice, as part of the fulfillment of the KM system. In this regard, within the Corporation, strategies articulated in each plan translate directly into department business plans through the annual business planning process. From an external perspective, the intention of the planning philosophy is that the plans will also guide the business planning of key destination stakeholders through a planned stakeholder engagement strategy.

At this stage, the knowledge gained through the planning process has been embedded through the linkages to the Corporation's business plans however it is too early to measure the extent of flow-on linkages with external industry stakeholders.

Technology

Technological infrastructure that enhances the gathering, storage and use of information. The technological infrastructure in the organisation is extensive and of high standard. Hence, the technology behind the gathering, storing and use of information was well supported. In practice, teams were allocated space on the organisation's shared computer storage system to store and freely access data and information. At a practical level teams also had unfettered access to the Internet, computers, data projectors and other equipment to assist with information management. As a result ready access to the organizations rich technological resource base greatly enhanced the gathering, storage and use of information.

Technological infrastructure that facilitates knowledge creation, embodiment and dissemination and use. As outlined above, technological resources were such that the process of knowledge-building and embodiment was well supported. The complexities of knowledge creation and embodiment in this case were such, however, that the process could have been better supported through a more sophisticated data base design, that allowed teams to better track their work, monitor progress and progressively build each plan.

With regard to dissemination, the development phase of the project culminated with the implementation of a dedicated website for each destination, complete with the completed plan and supporting research data, contacts and relevant information. Each web site is designed to provide stakeholders and interested parties with ready access to destination information and knowledge in an attempt to enhance understanding and decision-making.

Technological infrastructure that enhances communication, collaboration and decision making. Direct access to email and telecommunications allowed regular contact between project management, team leaders and team members. At a formal level, regular electronic bulletins and newsletters kept teams and senior management informed of progress and issues. Minutes of meetings, key project decisions and input on important issues were also facilitated this way. Overall, the technological infrastructure was sufficient to effectively manage administrate communications, but as pointed out above, at the team level more could have been done to better facilitate collaboration and knowledge-building through more sophisticated project software design.

Content

Availability of data and information that is relevant, accurate, current and of appropriate quality. Due to the organisation's considerable resources there was no shortage of quality data and information from which the teams could draw on to develop each plan. As the project proceeded, information gaps became more apparent and significantly, the deficient state of the organisation's data, information and knowledge management process was exposed. Currency of research data became an issue with critical performance reports needing to be updated several times over the course of planning.

Overall, although there were the considerable resources available, the inadequacy of information and knowledge management systems suggests that the planning process could have been enhanced through the creation of an information and knowledge map (Awad and Ghaziri 2004) to better identify, locate and assess the availability, quality and relevance of data and information.

Continuous Improvement

Capability of the organisation to monitor performance and reflect on practice and experience. While performance measures are a mandatory aspect of business planning, mechanisms that focus on the monitoring of and reflection on experience are not well developed in the organisation. Major projects and programs are monitored on a regular basis and procedural adjustments and refinements made as necessary but a more considered approach of pause and reflection on deeper experience is not characteristic of the business culture. This issue was highlighted in the planning process where, despite the many planning and review meetings convened to deal with immediate problems or issues, little time was spent processing performance and experience to any depth. Similarly the experience gained from developing the draft plans did not seem to greatly inform the review process and development of the final documents. On reflection, the pressures to carry out the task of DMP planning in addition to daily operational responsibilities appeared to inhibited the organisation's capacity to set aside the time and space needed to monitor and reflect on experience in a more considered way.

Capability of the organisation to apply learning in practice as an ongoing process of improvement. Throughout the DMP planning process regular internal review and feedback sessions were undertaken to monitor progress and address issues and concerns arising. Regular sessions were conducted with management, team leaders and team members, and outcomes directly fed into the ongoing refinement of methodology and project coordination. On a number of occasions issues arose that required intervention in team structure, group dynamics, planning processes and timelines, stakeholder engagement and the structure of the plan itself. In a practical sense, learning gained from experience fed directly into the refinement of the program. As indicated above however most of this learning and improvement occurred at the shallow or procedural end of the knowledge spectrum. With mechanisms and support in place to consider and reflect on deeper experience, the planning process could have been richer and the transition from draft to completed plans may have been more effective. A commitment to the application of learning as part of an ongoing process of continuous improvement will greatly enrich the next phase of stakeholder engagement and review.

DISCUSSION

The first factor in the framework raises the salient issue of goal alignment. In applying this principle to the case study, the discussion indicates that knowledge management principles were applied early in the planning cycle and this promoted synergy between corporate and strategic planning goals. This ensured that the purpose of the planning exercise was in consistent with corporate aspirations and that outcomes would contribute to overall corporate performance. In this regard the case study reinforces the importance of goal alignment as a foundation element in planning exercises and as valid aspect of the assessment framework

The second factor in the framework points to the importance of a planning approach that seeks to balance top-down with bottom-up planning perspectives. In this case, the linear logical steps of the rational planning model were juxtaposed against an internal multi-functional team approach to planning, together with some level of consultation with external stakeholders. While the extent of external consultation remains a debatable issue, the case study indicates an endeavour to strive for a balance where the strategic intentions of the exercise are informed by a process orientated approach that encourages broadly based input, knowledge building, sharing, creativity, learning, and new ideas. Within the context of contemporary perspectives of knowledge based strategic planning, this factor of the framework appears quite valid as a means by which organisational capability can be measured or enhanced. Measured against this factor, the case may be deemed to be only partially successful.

The third factor of the framework raises key issues about an organisation's capacity to implement a knowledge management agenda. Here the framework focuses on critical aspects of an organisation's fitness to successfully undertake planning from a knowledge-based perspective. The discussion highlights the strengths and weaknesses of the planning exercise in terms of leadership, process, people and culture, technology, content and continuous improvement. Through the discussion it becomes apparent that the capacity of the organisation in each area is variable and that, on reflection, more could have been done to improve performance in each area. In this regard, this aspect of the framework is also considered most valid in assessing organisational capability, underlining critical aspects of organisational capacity.

Overall the case study highlights the usefulness of the framework as a tool for analysing organisational capability and as a point of reference for planners preparing for specific knowledge based planning projects. It highlights the salient factors to be considered for the successful implementation of planning programs, irrespective of the size or scale of an organisation and the extent of its access to resources. Further, primary research will likely refine the elements of the framework and strengthen its validity as a planning and assessment tool.

In summary, findings support that an organisation's ability to develop sustainable competitive advantage through knowledge resources and dynamic capabilities is inextricably linked to the organisation's ability to implement a KM agenda. Firstly it promotes greater awareness of and the need for alignment between corporate goals and project goals to ensure that planning is consistent with overall corporate aspirations. In this particular case, as principles of knowledge management were applied at the beginning of the planning cycle, there was complete synergy. Secondly, the framework points clearly to the importance of a planning approach that seeks to achieve a balance between classical and emergent perspectives, in order to enhance the prospects of gaining and sustaining a competitive advantage in complex business environments. In this case example, while gaining a competitive advantage over other organisations was not an overt goal of the exercise; implicit in corporate and project aspirations is the aim to enhance the competitiveness of the State's destinations. More important perhaps, from a process perspective, is the need to foster an approach that is cognisant and inclusive of all key stakeholder interests. In this regard the project did not initially take an all-encompassing view of stakeholder input, in preference to a staged process of engagement over time—which is still underway. Whether this proves to be a prudent or successful approach remains to be seen but importantly the framework points to the need to consider this aspect as a strategic planning issue.

Finally, in the literature, most analysis is based on individual organisations. However, in this paper the analysis examines the interaction of more complex ad-hoc groups within the organisation. This raises issues of power and politics within the firm which serve to complicate the analysis and have been ignored in many prior studies.

This paper has underlined the value of linkages between knowledge and knowledge management in strategic planning and highlighted the issue of the capacity of organisations to implement knowledge management agendas. A theoretical framework for assessing the capability of organisations to implement knowledge based strategic planning programs is developed which, when applied to a case study, stands up as a useful tool for analysis. Despite the acknowledged limitations, the paper recommends the framework as a tool for analysing organisational capability and as a point of reference for planners preparing for specific knowledge based strategic planning projects.

RERERENCES

Awad, E., and Ghaziri, H. 2004. *Knowledge Management*. Pearson Education, New Jersey.

Barney, J. 1986. Organisational culture: can it be a source of sustained competitive advantage. *Academy of Management Review*, Volume 11, Number 3, pp. 656-665.

Cooper, C. 2005. *Managing Tourism Knowledge: Concepts and Approaches*. Channel View Publications, Clevedon, UK.

Denison, D.R. and Mishra, A.K. 1995. Toward a theory of organisational culture and effectiveness. *Organisational Science*. Volume 6, Number 2, pp. 204-223.

Drew, S. 1999. Building knowledge management into strategy: making sense of a new perspective. *Long Range Planning*, Volume 32, Number 1, pp. 130-136.

Eisenhardt, M.K., and Martin, J.A. 2000. Dynamic capabilities: what are they? *Strategic Management Journal*, Volume 21, pp. 1105-1121.

Gilmore, W.S., and Camillus, J.C. 1996. Do your planning processes meet the reality test? *Long Range Planning*, Volume 29, Number 6, pp. 869-879.

Grant, R. M. 1997. The knowledge-based view of the firm: implications for management practice. *Long Range Planning*, Volume 30, Number 3, pp. 450-454.

Hill, C.W.L., Jones, G.R., and Galvin, Peter. 2004. *Strategic Management–An Integrated Approach*. John Wiley and Sons, Australia.

Hofstede, G. 1986. The usefulness of the "organizational culture" concept. *Journal of Management Studies, 23*, 253-257.

Kakabadse, N.K., Kouzmain, A., Kakabadse, A. 2001. From tacit knowledge to knowledge management: leveraging invisible assets. *Knowledge and Process Management*, Volume 8. Number 3, pp. 137-154.

Knight, T., and Howes, T. 2003. *Knowledge Management–A Blueprint for Delivery*. Butterworth-Heinemann, Oxford, UK.

Mintzberg, H. 1994. The fall and rise of strategic planning. *Harvard Business Review*, January-February, pp. 107-114.

Nonaka and Takeuchi 1995 In Awad, E., and Ghaziri, H. 2004. *Knowledge management*. Pearson Education, New Jersey.

Porter, M.E. 1996. What is strategy? *Harvard Business Review*, November-December, pp. 61-78.

Quintas, P., Lefrere, P., and Jones, G. 1997. Knowledge management: A strategic agenda. *Long Range Planning*, Volume 30, Issue 3, June, pp. 385-391.

Standards Australia. 2003. *Interim Australian Standard, Knowledge Management*. Standards Australia International Ltd., NSW.

Teece, D.J., Pisano, G., Shuen, A. 1997. Dynamic capabilities and strategic management. *Strategic Management Journal*, Volume 18:7, pp. 509-533.

Tiwana, A. 2000. *The Knowledge Management Toolkit*. Prentice Hall PTR, New Jersey.

Tourism Queensland. 2001. *TQ Corporate Plan 2001–2005*. Tourism Queensland, Brisbane.

Tourism Queensland. 2003. *Tourism Queensland Corporate Planning*. Tourism Queensland, Brisbane.

Tourism Queensland. 2004a. *Destination Management Plan*. Tourism Queensland, Brisbane.

Wikland, J., Shepherd, D. 2003. Knowledge-based resources, entrepreneurial orientation, and the medium sized business. *Strategic Management Journal*, Volume 24, pp. 1307-1314.

Wittington, R. 1993. *What is Strategy–and does it Matter?* Routledge, London and New York.

doi:10.1300/J162v07n01_07

European Spa World:
Chances for the Project's Sustainability
Through Application
of Knowledge Management

Sonja Sibila Lebe

SUMMARY. In this paper, we describe an international project for developing 'Wellness Tourism' across four regions of central Europe. The paper examines this project from the viewpoint of knowledge management and the partnerships involved in this project. doi:10.1300/J162v07n01_08 *[Article copies available for a fee from The Haworth Document Delivery Service: 1-800-HAWORTH. E-mail address: <docdelivery@haworthpress.com> Website: <http://www.HaworthPress.com> © 2006 by The Haworth Press, Inc. All rights reserved.]*

KEYWORDS. Cross-border co-operation, wellness, European Spa World, Slovenia, Austria, Hungary, partnership, innovation

Sonja Sibila Lebe is Senior Lecturer, Faculty of Economics and Business, and Head of Tourism Department, Scientific Institute for Regional Development, University of Maribor, Slovenia. She is Project Leader for the Slovene part of the European Spa World Project (E-mail: SonjaS.Lebe@uni-mb.si).

[Haworth co-indexing entry note]: "European Spa World: Chances for the Project's Sustainability Through Application of Knowledge Management." Lebe, Sonja Sibila. Co-published simultaneously in *Journal of Quality Assurance in Hospitality & Tourism* (The Haworth Hospitality Press, an imprint of The Haworth Press, Inc.) Vol. 7, No. 1/2, 2006, pp. 137-146; and: *Knowledge Sharing and Quality Assurance in Hospitality and Tourism* (ed: Noel Scott and Eric Laws) The Haworth Hospitality Press, an imprint of The Haworth Press, Inc., 2006, pp. 137-146. Single or multiple copies of this article are available for a fee from The Haworth Document Delivery Service [1-800-HAWORTH, 9:00 a.m. - 5:00 p.m. (EST). E-mail address: docdelivery@haworthpress.com].

Available online at http://jqaht.haworthpress.com
© 2006 by The Haworth Press, Inc. All rights reserved.
doi:10.1300/J162v07n01_08

INTRODUCTION

In 2002, the Austrian regions of Styria and Burgenland invited their neighbour countries; Slovenia and Hungary to participate in an INTERREG project concerning wellness tourism. In an INTERREG project, the European Union (EU) grants up to 75% of the funds to support promising projects that are dedicated to stimulating cross-border co-operation among border regions of EU member countries. The aim of this funding is to accelerate economic growth in less-privileged border regions. The Austrian partners prepared the idea and the draft for the project. Two years later, Slovenia prepared a mirror project, and Hungary followed with its mirror project in 2005.

In continental Europe, 'wellness tourism' is used to describe a product based on four main pillars: (1) Physical activities–fitness programs as well as indoor and outdoor recreation; (2) Vital cuisine–based on supreme foods, quite often gained through biodynamic land cultivation, prepared in a vitamin and mineral friendly way, which also is "plaisir des yeux" (pleasure for the eyes) when served to the guests; (3) Programs for "pampering" guests, such as several kinds of saunas (Finnish sauna, Hammam–the Turkish sauna, infra-red sauna etc.), relaxation rooms with soft, meditative music, different types of massages, often combined with alternative medicine treatments such as Wai-Thai, Reiki, Shiatsu, Ayurveda or alternative medicine therapies such as aromatherapy, cromotherapy (colours), thalassotherapy (salt water) etc.; and (4) Leisure–including programs providing "food for the soul," including cultural events, animation for adults and children, excursions, getting to know the local way of living etc. on the one hand, and esoteric programmes, including rooms for meditation, courses with spiritual content, well-being counselling, well-being educational literature available, special wellness on-site events such as dance classes taught by renowned dance teachers etc. on the other (Evans, 2000; Gojcic, 2005). Wellness tourism is said to have a good market potential, as it fits into the newest global market trends. It suits the 50 + generation, which is going to be the strongest segment in the forthcoming decades (ITB 2005). Health and related topics, like wellness, will thus be one of the most relevant substances in the tourism offer of the next decades, as the main segment searching for this kind of service are the 50+ tourists.

Bringing together people from three nations was difficult. There was a lot of mistrust to be overcome. The people involved in the project could not understand each other as they use three absolutely different languages: German–a Germanic language, Slovene–a Slavonic language and Hungarian–a Ugric-Finnish language). Additionally, these countries had until recently belonged to three different, partly hostile political systems (Austria as a parliamentary democracy, Hungary as a part of the orthodox communist Eastern Block regime, and Slovenia lying as a part of former Yugoslavia somewhere in-between the two systems, enjoying–compared to other communist regimes–a relatively large extent of political liberties).

Another difficulty was the unequal financial participation of the three co-operating regions. The Austrian region had been very successful in attracting about 3 million Euros from European and national funds. However, Slovenia and Hungary together did not collect even a quarter of that sum. Despite this it was crucial for the project that the four regions act as four equal partners (at least concerning all kinds of decision making on the future of the project). If this condition had not been fulfilled, Slovenia and Hungary would not have agreed to co-operate and consequently the Austrian partners could not have attracted the funds.

A solution was found through compromise. While decisions were made jointly, the Austrian partners got more space for promotion in catalogues and brochures, corresponding to the percentage of their financial participation. This allowed the European Wellness Project, the biggest (to date) tourism upgrade project in Europe to proceed. Its main goal was to link countries across borders in order to foster regional economies through developing and marketing wellness tourism. More specifically, the project creates, through aggressive marketing campaigns, an image for the region of being the heart of the European quality wellness market.

INITIATING THE EUROPEAN WELLNESS PROJECT (EWP) AND ITS ORGANISATIONAL STRUCTURE

All four regions have a common project leader. The headquarters of the EWP is located in Styria, as this region was the initiator of the project. Each one of the four regions has its own regional co-ordination structure which is financed out of regional funds. The members are mostly enterprises offering wellness programmes, as well as some regional and local tourism organisations. The project management costs are kept very low–less than 10% of the integral budget. Some 75% of the funds arised are targeted for marketing activities and 25% for project development (Steckbrief EWP, 2002).

Appointment of delegates to the EWP organisation is based on different principles across the four partners. Burgenland is represented by its regional tourist organisation, which is financing the project without the participation of enterprises instead deriving funds from regional and EU budgets. Hungary and Styria are represented by a mixed delegation comprised of members of the regional tourism organisation and tourism enterprises, corresponding to their financial participation in the project. Slovenia is represented exclusively by tourism enterprises.

The expectations, concerns and intensity and willingness to participate in the project vary considerably. In Slovenia, where private enterprise is active, these enterprises want to be involved in decision-making on all crucial issues, bringing their own ideas on what to do and how to manage the common future plans. The influence of enterprises from other regions is less intense, and ranges from moderate to insufficient.

When starting this project, a "concrete" proposal had to be presented to the participating enterprises in order to gather support. The two common activities that the parties could agree on at the start were to develop a brand for the joint region and to issue a catalogue. These activities also initiated a feeling of "belonging together" among partners. The EWP delegates agreed on the brand "European Spa World" followed by a claim "Borderless well-being." The word "wellness" was thus consciously excluded from the brand—firstly because it is not used in Romanic and English speaking countries to describe this kind of offer, and secondly, because it has become overused: it can even be found on tea bags, on polyester made clothing etc. The name "European Spa World" was designed to communicate the idea of up-market quality through the use of the word *spa*. "Spa" was found to have a triple meaning. The first meaning is as an abbreviation for sanum per aquam–health through water. The second is a name for all resorts with thermal water, and the third one is used worldwide to describe the offer in up-grade tourism establishments.

SYSTEM "DESTINATION WELLNESS"

The four regions involved in the EWP have plenty of geographic similarities. The landscape is characterised by cultivated, rolling hills. This part of Central Europe is a region of extended vineyards and excellent wines. Its surface combines two major European geographic entities: the pre-Alpine world and the great Pannonian plain. At its juncture the earth's surface is very thin, which leads to thermal springs that are used for the spa offer.

Several definitions of tourism destination management exist (Bieger, 2002). Nevertheless, it seems agreed in the literature that the term destination denotes an optimally united and market-oriented area in which, by developing important and dominant features or attributes, superior tourism performance is achieved in the long run in comparison to that of the competition (Margas and Jurdana-Smolcic 2005). To manage the complex socio-economic system called a tourism destination, and to facilitate creation of a tourism product and the marketing of the same, an organisation like a DMC (Destination Management Company) or DMO (Destination Marketing Organisation) is needed. Several models and definitions of such institutions and of destination management exist.

One of the best available ones and fully applicable to our case is the definition of Bieger (2002) who introduces a new approach to destination management. Instead of being oriented primarily to unique suppliers in the destination (important enterprises or groups, such as an association of restaurants or association of tourist farms etc.), his model is process-oriented. Bieger compares this approach with the process of re-engineering which reflects up to the HRD management of the DMO: instead of employing experts for the field of hospitality the DMO hires experts for the product level: snow-boarding, wellness, Nordic walking etc. These experts know best the wishes and needs of the users of "their" services and can thus perform an optimal service chain from the point of view of their target visitor segment. This approach (wellness programs as product) would suit very well for the project we are describing and would mean an innovative approach in binding together this heterogeneous destination.

ISSUES IN ESTABLISHING A "EUROPEAN SPA WORLD" DESTINATION

Need for Organization

A destination–whether rural, urban, national or international–is a very complex, dialectic system (Lebe, 2005). Different kinds and layers of relationships, interests and dependencies can be identified within a destination, as can several subsystems that depend on each other each having a different intensity of interrelations (Mulej et al. 2000). The multiplicity of connections and relations existing between the organizations involved in a regional economic and/or social system are neither random nor chaotic (Blazevic & Jelusic 2005). Destinations as dialectic systems can be successfully managed if the subsystems and their inter-dependencies (relationships, partnerships) are adequately defined and consecutively organised. This usually leads to a reduction in a systems' complexity in order to make it operable and is achieved by focusing only on key subsystems and on the most important relationships in the destination. This also applies to the quality and extent of information flows among organizations. There is a need to understand how to iden-tify and focus on relevant information.

To assure a destination's success in a time of intense, global competi-tion, it needs to be financially and intellectually strong and unified. This means a destination management organization has to be created that is able to act on behalf of all stakeholders of the destination. The first task of such an organization is to define relationships and activities for both the internal operation of the system and activities that are perceived out-side the organisation as "services" offered to be purchased (Kovac 2002).

In a destination, several types of partnerships can be identified. Be-sides the more well-known public-private partnership, there may be several public-public and of private-private partnerships as well. These relationships are found in the ESW destination described here. Apart from the classical examples of relationships like distribution chains that are applicable to single enterprise and are managed by each firm indi-vidually (Kotler et al. 2003), other relationships need to be developed among special interest groups—one of them being a Destination Man-agement Organization (DMO). This involves some enterprises putting a part of their budget together for marketing in order to obtain synergy in performing activities that would be too expensive for an individual en-terprise. DMO members participate financially and through contribut-ing their knowledge. Expert partnerships (like the EWP) can bring additional benefits such as data unification and simplification and a stronger position in negotiations with suppliers or purchasers. A splen-did opportunity for synergy can be found in introducing quality stan-dards for the whole destination or by organising common training programmes for employees—both important organisational innovations.

Need to Consider 'Culture'

Cross-cultural research in tourism is receiving increasing attention from academics. However, little has been done with regard to the assessment of cultural differences in tourist management (Kozak et al. 2003). The ESW project dealt with multi-cultural aspects of visitor satisfaction on at least three levels. The first level is building the interaction of the four regional partners having different economic backgrounds and cultures. This requires addressing several difficulties on the one hand (i.e. difficulties in negotiations to reach the agreement on how to act) and several benefits on the other (e.g. the Slovene partners shared their knowledge about the Italian and the Russian markets with their EWP partners; the Slovene partners took the lead in the sub-project of promoting the ESW on foreign markets that were absolutely new for the prevailing part of international partners).

Investing in intercultural studies and understanding each other better would help overcome the negative consequences of decades of political division. Although the project began in 2003, trust has taken time to develop and the continuation of the project after the state-aid phase is finished is not assured. For some members, the financially dominant Austrian provinces may be perceived as a threat. This perception is encouraged by a lack of language skills by some delegates leading to a negative effect on the perceived equality of the project partners.

A second area at the micro level within the participating enterprises concerns the relationships between the destination 'management' and employees. A problem encountered in all four regions (and typical for European tourism generally) is a shortage of highly skilled personnel in some crucial professions (like waiters) who are being "imported" from Eastern European countries into the countries of the EU. This leads to problems since the service provided can only be good if they are pleased with their work, their salary and, of course, with their environment, including relationships to other colleagues. Quite often, language barriers have to be overcome in the first weeks or months of their engagement–but later, it is exactly the knowledge of the mother tongue that makes this employee interesting and appropriate for the enterprise as communicators for their own native language guests.

A third relationship is between the customers and the employees. In the EU, over 20 languages are spoken, and many more regional cultures can be clearly differentiated. Enterprises that employ people from abroad have advantages if they integrate international employees into the process of product/service creation and direct contact with costumers. Tourists are normally happy finding in the hotel someone who understands them, who knows about their expectations and habits and is able to meet their requirements. Integrating these employees consciously into the "visible" part of the offer would represent an innovative way of adding value to the wellness project ("all-round well-being" through tailor-made offer in one's mother tongue).

A Destination as a Knowledge-Bound, Competitive and Innovation-Friendly System

In the 1980 a common view was that competitive advantage was based upon the competitive positioning of the organisation (here destination) and this was derived upon systematic planning (Evans et al., 2003). This period corresponds to the foundation of strong national tourism organisations, which carried out extended marketing campaigns in order to set up a desired image of national destinations and their stakeholders.

Nowadays destinations are seen to require knowledge as a source of competitive advantage. Destinations with a poor level of destination knowledge management usually concentrate on marketing campaigns and neglect other vital, knowledge-bound aspects of destination management. The biggest opportunity for international projects such as the ESW is in putting together experiences, knowledge and skills that are accumulated in respective different regions and different cultures. If partners decide to work together with the aim of consciously allocating (and marketing) region-specific services, based on knowledge that derives from regional traditions, they can achieve a very high level on innovative and unique business solutions that can practically impossibly be replicated–surely the best possible competitive advantage.

Special regard should hereby be dedicated to the question how to market this unique offer. The important change, with its paradigm shift towards the experience economy, which took place in modern economy, should urgently be taken into account. It can be best seen in the innovative kind of engaging the customer through experiences, rather than just servicing. In this way, it helps creating value in an increasingly competitive business environment (Knutson and Beck 2003) and is indispensable when setting strategic decisions, such as the vision, the mission, the strategy and the firm's (destination's) USP (unique selling proposition). We argue that this new attitude is especially important in the field of services where tourism belongs.

CONCLUSION

This article has described an international tourism project begun in 2002 which is approaching its final stage (the co-financing will expire by the end of 2006). It has examined creation of competitive advantage through innovation in wellness tourism. At the start of this four-region project, its aim was to establish a quality destination brand for the international tourism market, based on a health tourism offering. This project has improved the position of the four regions through improved marketing efficiency. The central point of article examines different layers of partnerships within a new destination and the problems these cause. The problems experienced in this project range from a lack of a common language to inclusion of different stakeholders. The future of this unique partnership is in further development of creative joint activities, such as common educational and training programmes. Knowledge sharing of the experiences of single partners in the system is required to best integrate the local traditions into shaping the offer, and for better knowledge of each other's offer. This more intensive co-operation can show additional possibilities of linking outside the tourism sector for creating a better, more sophisticated and thus a more competitive offer, e.g., in the fields of leisure, (alternative) medicine, psychology, sociology etc.

Further knowledge sharing is required in how to develop systematic plans for penetrating new markets using the knowledge of unique partners that have already gathered valuable experience in those markets. There is a need to further develop sentiment about "our project" and "us as partners" among the four regions and this feeling of pride transmitted to project partners. This is a further key step for this unique project, joining absolutely different languages, cultures and traditions into a new geographical entity–a wellness destination. This sense of unity is required as a means of internal marketing and to be clearly transmitted in all promotional messages and in all other kinds of communication with all the relevant publics. If this can be achieved then the aim of the project, to implement high-level marketing, would thus be fulfilled.

REFERENCES

Bieger, Thomas: Management von Destinationen. 5., Neu bearbeitete und ergaenzte Auflage. 2002 R. Oldenbourg Verlag Muenchen Wien.

Blazevic, Branko and Adriana Jelusic: Estimating model parameters and the model of regional economic development. 2005: The 13th WOSC international congress on cybernetics and systems. (Volume 9, Tourism cybernetics. Pages 95-104) University of Maribor, Faculty of Economics and Business.

Cho, Dong-Sung and Hwy-Chang Moon: From Adam Smith to Michael Porter. Evolution of Competitiveness Theory. 2000 World Scientific Publishing, Singapore.

Evans, Mark: Wellness. Therapien fuer natuerliche Gesundheit und Wohlbefinden. 2000 Eurobooks Cyprus Ltd, Limasol.

Evans, Nigel; Campbell, David; Stonehouse, David: 2003 Strategic Management for Travel and Tourism., Butterworth Heinemann.

Gojcic, Slavka: Wellness. 2005, Zalozba GV Ljubljana.

ITB 2005: Matthias Horx Insitute's study on global trends and their impact on tourism.

Knutson, Bonnie, Jeffrey A. Beck: 2003 Identifying the Dimensions of the Experience Construct: Development of the Model. JQAT, Vol. 4, No. 3/4.

Kotler, Philip; Bowen, John; Markens, James: Marketing for Hospitality and Tourism, 2003, Prentice Hall.

Kovac, Jure: Network organizations. 2002 Management, Vol. 7 (1), pages 51-65).

Kozak, Metin; Enrique Bigné, Luisa Andreu: Limitations of Cross-Cultural Customer Satisfaction Research and Recommending Alternative Methods. 2003 JQAHT, Vol. 4, 3/4.

Lebe, Sonja Sibila: Possible way of sustainable tourism development in rural areas by innovating its organisation through network management. 2005: The 13th WOSC international congress on cybernetics and systems. (Volume 9, Tourism cybernetics. Pages 47-57) University of Maribor, Faculty of Economics and Business.

Magaš, Dragan; Dora Smolcic-Jurdana: The tourist destination as a socio-economic system. 2005: The 13th WOSC international congress on cybernetics and systems. (Volume 9, Tourism cybernetics. Pages 7-17) University of Maribor, Faculty of Economics and Business.

Mulej, Matjaz and co-authors: Dialekticna in druge mehkosistemske teorije. Podlaga za celovitost in uspeh managementa. 2000, Ekonomsko-poslovna fakulteta Univerze v Mariboru.

Page, Steven: Tourism Management: Managing for Change. 2003 Butterworth Heinemann.

Persic, Milena; Cetinski, Vinka; Stanicic, Kristijan: Integrated Tourism Destination Quality Management & Information Needs (Case Study: "The Rivijera of Opatija"), 2005: The 13th WOSC International Congress on Cybernetics and Systems. (Volume 9, Tourism Cybernetics. Pages 95-104) University of Maribor, Faculty of Economics and Business.

Selin, S. W., & Chavez, D. (1995). Developing an evolutionary tourism partnership model. Annals of Tourism Research, 22(4), 814-856.

Steckbrief EWP. 2002, Steirische Tourismus GmbH Graz.

doi:10.1300/J162v07n01_08

The Tourism Intelligence Network:
The Quebec Source for Information
on the Evolving Tourism Industry

Sophie Lemelin

SUMMARY. This case study examines the organisation of research in Quebec. It presents an example of best practice in tourism research dissemination. doi:10.1300/J162v07n01_09 *[Article copies available for a fee from The Haworth Document Delivery Service: 1-800-HAWORTH. E-mail address: <docdelivery@haworthpress.com> Website: <http://www.HaworthPress.com> © 2006 by The Haworth Press, Inc. All rights reserved.]*

KEYWORDS. Knowledge, tourism, networks, Quebec

Sophie Lemelin holds a bachelor degree in Management of Tourism at the University of Quebec in Montreal (UQAM) and in 2005 conducted a comparative study about the governance of tourism between Quebec and Queensland for the Canadian Chair in Tourism. She now works for the Quebec Youth Tourism Organisation and still collaborates with the Tourism Intelligence Network. She is an active member of the UQAM Management Network and plans to start a Master degree in project management next year (E-mail: lemelin.sophie.3@courrier.uqam.ca).

The author would like to acknowledge advice and editing provided by Dr. Noel Scott from The University of Queensland.

[Haworth co-indexing entry note]: "The Tourism Intelligence Network: The Quebec Source for Information on the Evolving Tourism Industry." Lemelin, Sophie. Co-published simultaneously in *Journal of Quality Assurance in Hospitality & Tourism* (The Haworth Hospitality Press, an imprint of The Haworth Press, Inc.) Vol. 7, No. 1/2, 2006, pp. 147-159; and: *Knowledge Sharing and Quality Assurance in Hospitality and Tourism* (ed: Noel Scott and Eric Laws) The Haworth Hospitality Press, an imprint of The Haworth Press, Inc., 2006, pp. 147-159. Single or multiple copies of this article are available for a fee from The Haworth Document Delivery Service [1-800-HAWORTH, 9:00 a.m. - 5:00 p.m. (EST). E-mail address: docdelivery@haworthpress.com].

Available online at http://jqaht.haworthpress.com
© 2006 by The Haworth Press, Inc. All rights reserved.
doi:10.1300/J162v07n01_09

INTRODUCTION

Sharing tourism knowledge has recently emerged as one of the most important issues for many destinations. Research is now considered as a prerequisite for better planning and product development in tourism research centres, and research units within tourism organisations have become common as managers seek to foster their company and destination's competitiveness. Links with academia are being viewed less cynically by industry stakeholders and indeed are now seen as a source of knowledge.

A focus on knowledge sharing is particularly important for tourism destinations. A destination may be considered as a network of organisations and stakeholders (Cooper and Scott, 2005). Within this network, conception of shared knowledge creates competitive advantage. While producing new tourism knowledge and innovation is important, destinations have to ensure the dissemination and sharing of knowledge in order to maximize this competitive advantage for their stakeholders.

The Importance of Managing Knowledge

A review of the literature of management indicates that managing the creation of knowledge and management is a critical issue at the businesses level(Choi & Cho, 2000; Cooper, 2005; Quintas, Lefrere, & Jones, 1997; Whitehill, 1997). The space industry, the computer industry as well as the biotechnology industry have been using this strategy for years (Gupta and McDaniel, 2002) where successful corporations have dedicated research and development (R & D) departments. By collecting, analysing data and then, producing relevant information, R & D units have created useable knowledge and competitive success. Those able to transform and explain such information reach a better level of decision-making(Cooper, 2002; Hardy, Phillips, & Lawrence, 2003; Roos & Roos, 1997; von Krogh, Nonaka, & Aben, 2001). In the long term, those businesses will succeed amidst the competitiveness of the industry.

Arguably, the tourism industry faces a more complex reality than an individual business. The international reality of tourism leads to competitiveness at the destination level, which requires consultation, collaboration and strong relationships between stakeholders. Technology, coopetition and the globalization lead tourism businesses to provide opportunities for sharing of knowledge within a destination cluster, growing overall visitors, rather than competing directly. But the competitive nature of tourism within a destination can reduce the creation of shared knowledge (Cooper and Scott, 2005).

Producing and distributing knowledge within a destination cluster helps to better plan for the future, a basic first step to increasing competitiveness as a destination. While knowledge can't guarantee immediate success, it can at least reduce the risk of bad decision-making. Thus, a knowledge sharing strategy is the key to maintaining a competitive advantage (Ritchie, 2005).

Busy with daily operations, tourism businesses don't have the time for long term planning based on internal research. The lack of time, the scarcity of financial resources and the rareness of qualified human resources contribute to bad decision-making based upon intuition. In addition, an overabundance of information can easily confuse small and medium sized enterprises managers. To be really understood, information needs to be explained and it is a real challenge to filter a large amount of data into relevant information (Peloquin, 2005). This paper provides a case study of knowledge sharing within the Quebec tourism industry and illustrates the value of knowledge and importance of sharing knowledge.

The Quebec Tourism Industry and Knowledge Creation

In the Quebec tourism industry, research has not until recently been a focus for collaborative effort. Compared to other destinations visited as part of this research[1] but not discussed, the Quebec tourism industry did not, until 2004, have access to competitive public knowledge. Tourisme Québec, the peak marketing body, does conduct timely research providing statistics of tourist visitation, accommodation occupancy and other competitiveness indicators. It also supports research initiatives from the industry by financing specific studies as well as giving mandates for research into special interest. However, Tourisme Québec did not provide intelligence tourism to the industry but concentrates its effort on more traditional research. On its side, intelligence gathering is done constantly, with a long-term perspective. It covers a variety of major topics. Findings are published at regular intervals in the form of short analyses.

This context led the Quebec Tourism Industry, in 2004 to support and implement the Quebec Tourism Intelligence Network. The role of this public organisation's works is to provide the Quebec industry with a holistic knowledge based in order to increase the industry's operations and enhance its competitiveness. The role of this organisation was based on reducing the within cluster competitiveness of the Quebec tourism industry by creating public knowledge and disseminating it to the entire industry. In this context, Tourisme Québec still invests in some research projects and the TIN, becomes a complement to what is done already for the industry.

Officially created in January 2004, the Tourism Intelligence Network (TIN) was launched in May of the same year by the Chair in Tourism at the Université du Québec à Montréal (UQAM) School of Business Administration. The Chair itself was established in January 1992 through a partnership between Tourisme Québec and the UQAM. Its involvement in the industry, numerous publications and various informative activities make the Chair in Tourism a rich source of knowledge for tourism stakeholders. In addition, many students and university graduates gain practical experience by participating in its research projects and organized events. As its most recent initiative, the TIN complements the Chair's mission: "to foster the growth and prestige of the Quebec tourism industry by supporting research, the dissemination of information and education."

Origins and Approach

The Tourism Intelligence Network (TIN) grew out of a suggestion put forth in the 1998 Quebec tourism policy[2] and meets a vital industry need that is still central to the new policy. The TIN is an innovative industry tool, based on a structured procedure for gathering and analyzing information. The TIN closely monitors changes in the tourism industry around the world, regularly producing short, 750 to 1000 word analyses with value-added information on topics of interest to Quebec decision-makers working in small and medium-sized businesses. This is accomplished by a team of three people working full-time and three others on a part time basis to gather and analyze information to identify threats, opportunities, issues, emerging trends, travel behaviour, strategies used by other destinations among other categories of knowledge. These analyses help decision-makers anticipate changes, discover and accommodate new consumer behaviours, identify new ways of doing things, use benchmarking(what is done elsewhere), and thus better fulfil tourists' expectations. Analyses are available free of charge on a Web site and are sent to over 10,000 subscribers via a bi-monthly e-newsletter.

Analysts working at the TIN use a variety of sources of market intelligence. From statistics to indicators, through research, plans and studies, the availability of large amounts of information requires a specific research question to be developed. They have to select relevant information by a continuous press review. A weekly editorial meeting allows staff to discuss the hottest topics and direct their writing to better supply the industry.

The QTIN offers a variety of services free of charge such as:

- Web site
- Bi-monthly intelligence newsletter
- Summaries of conferences
- Regional seminars
- Bibliographic reference service

It also offers billed services to respond to specific demands, such as:

- Benchmarking
- Customized intelligence gathering
- Documentation services

Intelligence is identified and monitored by three committees: The Management Committee, a Steering Committee and a Scientific Subcommittee. Each of them has a specific role and ensures the responsiveness of the TIN to the industry needs. The Management Committee is formed by the Chair in Tourism, the TIN director and one representative from each financial partner. The Steering Committee combines various influential stakeholders from the Quebec tourism industry, such as representatives from the regional tourism organisations and industry associations. Its role is to identify ongoing topics as well as selective topics. Ongoing topics cover several subjects such as products and activities, e-tourism, accessibility, management, etc. Ad hoc topics are pursued only for a limited time and include benchmarking of policies and programs instituted by other destination, profile and behaviours of clientele visiting Quebec (and, most importantly, those who do not visit Quebec) as well as emerging products and activities. The Scientific Subcommittee works to ensure the intelligence sources' validity and the processes' integrity.

The TIN is a network of several types of partners: financial partners, associated partners, research and information partners, and institutional partners as well as individual partners with the expert network. The network is funded under a partnership between government bodies: Tourisme Québec and Dévelopement économique du Canada (Economic development of Canada ministry). Also, two private enterprises are financially involved: Transat A.T., the leading integrated holiday travel group in Canada, and IBM Canada, for technological support of TIN activities. There are also agreements for data purchase and skills transfer with some of international tourism institutions such as the Ministry for Tourism in France. Furthermore, agreements for information sharing and knowledge dissemination are effective with organisation like Statistics Canada and more informal collaboration with other foreign organisation like IPK International.[3] Those partners generally supply regular activities of the TIN. There are also specific associations with different partners for specific research projects. For example, Loto-Québec, the government agency for lottery, recently became a partner. Their specific interest was to hire a professional who will be monitoring changes for the tourism and entertainment sector. Tourisme Montréal (the regional tourism organisation for the metropolis) also plans to use the same approach of employing a person through the TIN in order to focus on Urban Tourism.

The core of TIN's function is information dissemination. A Web site and a bimonthly newsletter have reported on more than 300 analyses since the TIN launch. All TIN dissemination is based on an electronic solution and there is neither published magazine nor information letters distributed. Twice a month, subscribers receive by email the newsletter by which they can read the summary of each analysis. Then, if the reader is interested in one of them, the only need is to click on the summary or the title to be lead to the Web site and get the complete text. In this way, subscribers can get an overview of the newsletter content and they can read the article of their choice.

Once the subscriber is on the Web site to read the analysis, he sees the complete range of topics offered with the scroll menu. To illustrate the depth of a particular topic, a screen capture of the related web page to the e-tourism topic is shown in Figure 1.

The main menu in Figure 1 shows a variety of sections. One of these sections is the Intelligence Theme and gives the possibility to read about articles related to the chosen topic such as products and activities, accommodation, accessibility and transport, e-tourism, management, marketing and technology. Once the topic is selected, the reader can find all the related analyses. In this example, the selection of e-tourism leads to an overview of analyses summaries treating about this subject. For now, the website has only few analyses translated in English but, plans to get them all done in the mid-term time. The site may be found at veilletourisme.ca

FIGURE 1. Screen Capture from the TIN Web Site Showing the Depth of One of the Intelligence Themes

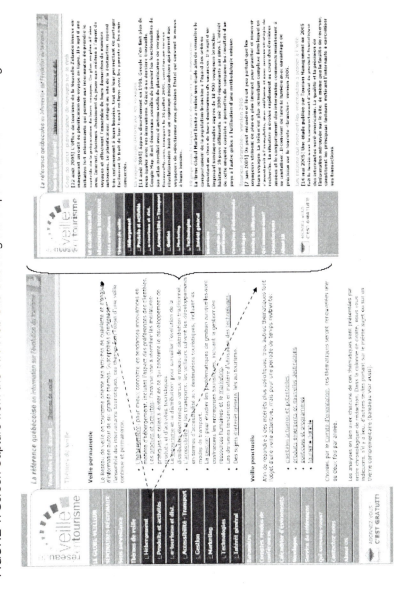

The TIN plans to visit and disseminate information to provinces stakeholders across the Quebec with a series of regional seminars. Those events aim to reach out directly more decision-makers, to make tourism players aware of the availability of intelligence, increase players' understanding about the industry issues specific to the region, and finally, to market the TIN and its services. Those seminars are organised in co-operation with regional associations and have, to date, visited two pilot regions. Through the financial support of Desjardins, a Quebec banking cooperative, the regional seminars series will be introduced into more regions in the next two years.

Clientele Profile

The dissemination of TIN benefits a number of sectors. A recent survey has been conducted by an independent market research company (ÉCHO sondage) to better understand the TIN clientele, their needs and interests. The methodology for this survey was separated in two phases. The first was an invitation to participate to the survey by email to all the subscribers. This email included a brief presentation of the study and the importance of their participation as well as a personal access code. A follow-up reminder was sent a week later. In all, 11425 people were contacted with 1063 invitations returned because of wrong addresses. Some 892 subscribers answered the survey, a response rate of 9%. However, there are approximately 3,000 active newsletter readers giving an active member response rate of approximately 30%.

The typical client is a woman from the Montreal region, aged between 35 and 45 and occupying a decision-making job within the hospitality sector. She has a degree and uses the internet more than once a day at work. Of the clients surveyed, 46% come from the tourism sector followed by 22% from the services sector defined as organisations offering consultation services, financial support to enterprises, advices about economic development or distribution network enterprises. Within the tourism sector, again half of the respondents work in the hospitality industry, whereas a quarter from the services sector is employed by economic development organisations.

The majority of the newsletter subscribers are decision-makers. Of this group, 31% are professionals, 19% are managers followed by 19% are owners or senior manager. The origin of respondents is mainly from the Quebec province and is shared as followed: 30% from the Montreal Region, 28% from the Montreal border regions, 17% from remote regions, 16% from the Quebec City region and 9% are from other Canadian provinces or other countries (mainly from France due to the TIN Web Site language barrier). Because of type of positions occupied by those surveyed, 68% have a university degree. A quarter have a technical level of studies and only 7% do not have a diploma.

A Network of Seasoned Experts and Contributors

The TIN also makes use of a solid network of experienced local, regional, national and international contributors and experts. Each one is a specialist. The individuals selected come from a variety of backgrounds: researchers and practitioners, working for associations, private enterprises or the public sector. Experts add to the prognostic value of the analyses written by staff researchers by contributing opinions on the possible outcome of a given situation and the likely consequences for the tourism industry. The TIN has around 15 experts around the world, collaborating on different projects and the relationship is bi-directional. The TIN responds to their request while experts comment some of our analyses.

National and International Renown

Both nationally and internationally, the Tourism Intelligence Network plays a leading role in the field of strategic intelligence. For example, both Morocco and Portugal have called on the TIN's expertise for help developing similar projects. In addition, France's Minister in charge of tourism has signed a partnership agreement with the Chair in Tourism concerning the transfer and exchange of strategic knowledge based on TIN research, an unusual step for a government body. In Canada, the Canadian Tourism Commission and the heads of various provincial tourism departments have expressed a keen interest in working with the TIN. In the words of one Tourism Ontarioofficial:"We're jealous of this Quebec project!"

Remarkable Results

Although online for less than a year, the Web site of this strategic intelligence service already boasts more than 300 analyses covering eight themes. The TIN team has also conducted surveys, taken part in five international conferences and developed a barometer describing the characteristics of the North American, French, British, German and Asian tourism markets.

The TIN's influence has snowballed: it has been quoted or its creators interviewed nearly 150 times in print and electronic media such as *La Presse* (a daily newspaper), TVA and Radio-Canada (television networks). Furthermore, it has had over 40 articles reprinted in whole or in part by magazines like *Les Affaires, Affaires Plus, l'Actualité* and *Magazine PME*, and it has contributed to the publications of approximately ten organizations as well as numerous in-house company newsletters. Also, the TIN has received last spring the National Silver Award for the Tourism Public organisation category gived by Tourisme Québec.

In addition, the survey has revealed a great responsiveness. It seems that the TIN has made a difference in the Quebec Tourism Industry. Indeed, 93% of people surveyed attest that the bimonthly newsletter helps them to increase their knowledge about different subjects. As well, 63% of them say that those analyses help to make better decisions and enhance the decision-making process. 54% of them say that those analyses influence their management practices.

Issues and Challenges for TIN

TIN faces some issues and challenges for many reasons. Its durability, its relevance and the quality of its work are crucial elements for the next two years. In fact, the TIN structure makes the organisation very precarious. This is a public service funded by public funds which makes its future funding uncertain. The agreement that created the TIN is a 3 year contract, so the TIN has to provide tangibles results to make their services vital for the industry.

Its funding structure is precarious but also provides credibility. At the beginning of the project, the TIN was planned to be part of Tourisme Québec. In this way, it would have been a real governmental research department. Perhaps this structure would have given stability, but it would have also involved more control from bureaucrats and state employee to the detriment of credibility and impartiality. Being an organisation on its own and independent by the university support gives the TIN a greater room for manoeuvre. The TIN must prove that its services are essential and by the very fact, that needs to have enough funds. Because of results obligations, the TIN has recently conducted a satisfaction survey among its members (as previously explained). Those results discussed previously provided one basis for evaluation of the TIN results.

The second issue faced by TIN concerns its utility to government. The perception is that "if the TIN stops its activities, the Quebec Tourism Industry won't fall." Tourist will still come and visit the province and the industry will continue to conduct its operations. This is why the TIN has sought to broaden its support from other industries. Beyond the tourism industry, TIN supplies information to analysts and research department within economic development organisation and banking institution. This expansion is supported by media coverage. This is increasing with the TIN director, the Chairman or a report analyst giving interviews that are widely reported. This has in turn benefited the Regional Seminars project. It has increased the number and diversity of its clientele.

The final crucial issue for TIN is linked to the quality of delivered services and its renewal. There is a continuous focus on responding to industry needs. As a public organisation, it must work for the members. To address this issue, the orientation committee works very closely with the TIN and, quarterly, the committee evaluate TIN work. Because this committee is formed by leading people from the industry, it ensures the validity and the relevance of TIN work. Also, because TIN is an electronic solution by disseminating essentially trough the Web site and the bi-monthly newsletter, members can evaluate reports in real time. This instant feedback from the readership, on the various articles indicates the subjects that have interested clientele, which ones has been less popular and how many people has read each one. To maintain the interest, the TIN renew its work by offering specific intelligence thematic. In this way, they are on the look-out for new trends and can easily respond to specific demands from the industry.

This flexibility and constant self-assessment and repositioning give the TIN a great advantage in addressing current issues and challenges. This way to manage the organisation helps to reach the objective of TIN which is creating and disseminating knowledge. In regards of the management methods and the client satisfaction results, TIN seems to make a difference by creating knowledge and gives the opportunity to the public to access it by a wide range of services.

CONCLUSION

Knowledge management is a well-recognized strategy for better decision-making. Being informed, businesses are aware of the possibilities and related consequences in the decision-making process. Thus, it becomes a competitive advantage to create and share knowledge. Knowledge management enables destinations to compete on the world market for a long period of time because they know (or can predict) what is going to happen. Because they took the time to analyse possibilities in the future, they are ready for any changes. This attitude makes them more proactive than reactive, and gives them an advantage compared to the others. For a destination, sharing this knowledge gives more power to single enterprises for decision-making. Thus, the addition of strong and unique enterprises gives a destination an advantage over its competitors.

The TIN is quite specific for the Quebec Tourism Industry. This organisation consolidates information to provide substantial analyses on relevant topics. One of the key components for knowledge management in Quebec is the dissemination. As a public organisation, the TIN serves all enterprises of the Quebec tourism Industry. Beyond its borders, TIN is constantly monitoring the industry in a long term perspective.

This case study is a great example of creating and sharing knowledge. The TIN renders tourism data, research and studies for the industry more accessible. The TIN is based on the concept that knowledge is a public good. Share it, disseminate it and the industry will experience a better cooperation as well as increase its competitiveness.

NOTES

1. During this research a number of research centres were visited in Australia. In one State, Queensland, over 15 research centres covering various subjects related to tourism were found. These centres examined topics from ecotourism to destination policy. Queensland research centres were found to play an important role in the tourism management within this State.

2. This document gives guidelines for the planning and the development of the Quebec tourism industry. One of the objectives was to endow the Quebec with a research center capable to supply up-to-date information, as well as to provide information dedicated to decisions-makers and small and medium-sized enterprises managers.

3. IPK International is a world Travel Monitor Company offering the largest premium data bank worldwide. It has been founded in 1969 in Germany. This company is an affiliate member of the World Tourism Organisation and the Pacific Asia Travel Association.

REFERENCES

Arsenault, M. Paul, (2005) Personal interview TIN Director, realised on 08/09/05.

Chair in Tourism (2002). *Corporate and Strategic Plan.* Montreal: Chair in Tourism, 1-12.

Choi, T. Y., & Cho, V. (2000). Towards a knowledge discovery framework for yield management in the Hong Kong hotel industry. *Hospitality Management, 19,* 17-31.

Cooper, C. (2002). Knowledge Management and Research Commercialisation Agendas. *Current Issues in Tourism, 5*(5), 375-377.

Cooper, C. (2005). *Managing Tourism Knowledge: Concepts and Approaches.* London: Channelview.

Cooper, C. & Scott, N. (2005). Knowledge for Networked Destinations. Paper submitted to the Recent Developments in Tourism Research Conference Faro. Portugal.

Dunn, D. & Salazar, A. (2004). Knowledge-based competitive advantage in the internet age: discovering emerging business strategies. *International Journal of Information Technology and Management (IJITM).* 3(2/3/4). 246-258.

Écho Sondage (2005). Confidential satisfaction survey on TIN services. Montreal: Écho Sondage, 1-78.

E. Hawkins, D. (2004). Transferring Tourism Knowledge. Paper submitted to the First World Conference on Tourism Communications (WTO). Spain. 1-13.

Hardy, C., Phillips, N., & Lawrence, T. B. (2003). Resources, Knowledge and Influence: The Organizational Effects of Interorganizational Collaboration. *Journal of Management Studies, 40*(2), 322-347.

Hölzl, B., Pechlaner, H., Tallinucci, V. (2004). Cross-level destination management and the transfer of knowledge. Paper submitted to the fifth European conference on Organizational Knowledge, Learning and Capabilities. Innsbruck. 1-20.

Kotelnikov, V. A (http: www.1000ventures.com accessed 08/01/05). (2002). Knowledge Management (KM): Collecting and Distributing both Explicit and Tacit Knowledge Throughout Your Organization.

Malhotra, Y. (interview with) (2003). Is knowledge the ultimate competitive advantage? *Business Management Asia,* Q3/4, 66-69.

Péloquin, M. Claude (2005), Personal interview, realised on 08/05/05.

Quintas, P., Lefrere, P., & Jones, J. (1997). Knowledge management: A strategic agenda. *Long Range Planning. 30*(3), 385-391.

Roos, G., & Roos, J. (1997). Measuring your Company's Intellectual Performance. *Long Range Planning, 30*(3), 413-426.

Ritchie, J. R. (2003). *The competitive destination: A sustainable tourism perspective.* CABI Pub., Oxon, UK. 1-52, 304 pages. Waldo Emerson, R. A (http://www.providersedge.com, accessed 08/01/05). (2003). The Providers Edge, LLC: The Knowledge Management Advantage.

Whitehill, M. (1997). Knowledge-based strategy to deliver sustained competitive advantage. *Long Range Planning, 30*(4), 621-627.

doi:10.1300/J162v07n01_09

Index

© 2006 by The Haworth Press, Inc. All rights reserved.

BOOK ORDER FORM!

Order a copy of this book with this form or online at:
http://www.HaworthPress.com/store/product.asp?sku= 5920

Knowledge Sharing and
Quality Assurance in Hospitality and Tourism

—— in softbound at $20.00 ISBN-13: 978-0-7890-3412-0 / ISBN-10: 0-7890-3412-3.
—— in hardbound at $38.00 ISBN-13: 978-0-7890-3411-3 / ISBN-10: 0-7890-3411-5.

COST OF BOOKS _____	❏ **BILL ME LATER:**
	Bill-me option is good on US/Canada/ Mexico orders only; not good to jobbers, wholesalers, or subscription agencies.
POSTAGE & HANDLING _____	
US: $4.00 for first book & $1.50 for each additional book	❏ **Signature** _____
Outside US: $5.00 for first book & $2.00 for each additional book.	❏ **Payment Enclosed: $**_____
SUBTOTAL _____	❏ **PLEASE CHARGE TO MY CREDIT CARD:**
In Canada: add 7% GST. _____	❏ Visa ❏ MasterCard ❏ AmEx ❏ Discover ❏ Diner's Club ❏ Eurocard ❏ JCB
STATE TAX _____	**Account #**_____
CA, IL, IN, MN, NJ, NY, OH, PA & SD residents please add appropriate local sales tax.	
FINAL TOTAL _____	**Exp Date**_____
If paying in Canadian funds, convert using the current exchange rate, UNESCO coupons welcome.	**Signature**_____
	(Prices in US dollars and subject to change without notice.)

PLEASE PRINT ALL INFORMATION OR ATTACH YOUR BUSINESS CARD

Name

Address

City   State/Province   Zip/Postal Code

Country

Tel   Fax

E-Mail

May we use your e-mail address for confirmations and other types of information? ❏Yes ❏No We appreciate receiving your e-mail address. Haworth would like to e-mail special discount offers to you, as a preferred customer.
We will never share, rent, or exchange your e-mail address. We regard such actions as an invasion of your privacy.

Order from your **local bookstore** or directly from
The Haworth Press, Inc. 10 Alice Street, Binghamton, New York 13904-1580 • USA
Call our toll-free number (1-800-429-6784) / Outside US/Canada: (607) 722-5857
Fax: 1-800-895-0582 / Outside US/Canada: (607) 771-0012
E-mail your order to us: orders@HaworthPress.com

For orders outside US and Canada, you may wish to order through your local
sales representative, distributor, or bookseller.
For information, see http://HaworthPress.com/distributors

(Discounts are available for individual orders in US and Canada only, not booksellers/distributors.)

Please photocopy this form for your personal use.
www.HaworthPress.com

BOF06